THE COMPLETE CONDUCTOR'S GUIDE
TO LABAN MOVEMENT THEORY

G-7184

THE COMPLETE CONDUCTOR'S GUIDE TO LABAN MOVEMENT THEORY

LISA A. BILLINGHAM

GIA Publications, Inc.
Chicago

G-7184

GIA Publications, Inc.
7404 South Mason Avenue
Chicago, IL 60638
www.giamusic.com

Copyright © 2009 GIA Publications, Inc.
All rights reserved.

Printed in the United States of America.

ISBN: 978-1-57999-697-0

For my parents.

Contents

Foreword by Bruce Chamberlain xi
Acknowledgments xiii
Introduction xv

CHAPTER 1: History 1
    Labanotation 6

CHAPTER 2: Body 9
    Experiencing the Patterns of Total Body Connectivity 12
        Breath 12
            Exercise 13
            Conducting Exercise 14
        Core-Distal Patterning 15
            Core-Distal Exercise 15
            Conducting Core-Distal Mirroring Exercise 16
            Exercise 17
        Head-Tail Patterning 17
            Head-Tail Exercise 18
        Upper-Lower Patterning 19
            Exercise: Seated Yield & Push 20
            Upper-Lower Exercise 22
    Grounding 22
        Body-Half Patterning 23
            Exercise in Body-Half Imagery 24
            Body-Half Exercise 1 25
            Body-Half Exercise 2 25
        Cross-Lateral Patterning 27
            Exercise: Tracing the Outer and
            Inner Connections 27
            Cross-Lateral Exercise Closing
            in Opposing Limbs 28
        Conclusion 29

　　　　　　Exercise for All Six Patterns
　　　　　　of Total Body Connectivity 30

CHAPTER 3: Effort 31
　　Effort. 31
　　Effort Elements 31
　　　　Flow. 31
　　　　Weight 32
　　　　Time 32
　　　　Space 34
　　　　Exercises: Exploration of the Effort Elements 34
　　　　　　Flow. 34
　　　　　　Weight 35
　　　　　　Time. 35
　　　　　　Space 36
　　Effort Elements in Combination 37
　　Effort Exercise: Effort Actions in Combination 38
　　Effort Exercise: Effort Actions in Pairs 40
　　　　Exercise: Using Your Dramatic Voice in Conversation. . 40
　　Complete Effort Actions and the Conducting Gesture 44
　　Conclusion 45

CHAPTER 4: Shape. 47
　　Shape. 47
　　Opening and Closing 48
　　　　Opening and Closing Exercise 49
　　　　Observing Opening and Closing Exercise 51
　　Shape Forms 52
　　Modes of Shape Change 53
　　Shape Flow 53
　　Directional 54
　　Carving 54
　　　　Exercise in Moving the Modes of Shape Change 54
　　Shape Flow Support 55
　　Shape Flow Qualities 56

  Exercise: Shape Flow Qualities in the
   Dimensional Cross of Axes. 56
 Applying Shape Flow Qualities to the Rehearsal. 58
 Conclusion 59

CHAPTER 5: Space 61
 Space. 61
 Gathering and Scattering 62
 Exercises. 62
  Gathering-Scattering. 62
  Holding-Releasing 63
  Clutching-Throwing 63
 Relationship to Conducting 64
 Kinesphere 65
  Observation Exercise 66
 Psychological Kinesphere. 66
 Approaches to Kinesphere 68
 Planes of the Body 69
 Exercises in Space Exploration with Global Rotation,
 Planes, and Breath. 70
  Cycling the Planes. 70
  Exercise in Global Joint Rotation 71
  Exercise: Cycling the Planes. 71
  Exercise for Connecting Breath to Movement 73
 Scales 73
 Dimensional Scale 74
  Dimensional Scale Exercise 75
 Symbols for the Body in Space. 77
 Exploration of Movement in the Cube 77
 Diagonal Scale 78

CHAPTER 6: Thematic Application 81
 Thematic Application of Laban Movement Analysis 81
 Inner-Outer. 82
  Journal Exercise in Inner-Outer 83

Stability-Mobility 83
Shape. 84
Stability-Mobility Using Body/Bartenieff Fundamentals. 85
    Breath Connectivity Exercise 85
    Core-Distal Connectivity 86
    Head-Tail Connectivity. 86
        Head-Tail Connection Exercise. 86
    Upper-Lower Connectivity 87
    Body-Half Connectivity 87
    Cross-Lateral Connectivity 87
    Exercise for Stability-Mobility Using Space Harmony . 88
    Diagonal Scale with Effort Elements in Combination . . 89
Function-Expression. 90
    Journal Exercise 90
Conclusion 91

Endnotes. 93
Bibliography 97
Index 101
About the Author. 106

Foreword
by Bruce Chamberlain

For most musicians, the name Rudolf Laban remains relatively unknown. This groundbreaking choreographer, movement analyzer, and teacher of movement developed a system of notation that depicts motions, not just static positions. This revolutionary system of three-dimensional terminology allows for the proportion of time. It is this intersection of movement analysis within the framework of proportional time that allows Laban's examinations of "movement choirs" and the concepts of "spatial harmonies" to resonate for all musicians and especially conductors. After all, a significant aspect of conducting is representing musical meaning through thoughtful gestural language.

Let the record reflect, however, that in the world of conducting pedagogy, I am an old dog. For more than thirty years I have had the elusive task of teaching conducting at the collegiate level. Students have ranged from the junior piano performance major who was convinced that he/she would never set foot in front of an ensemble, to doctoral choral conducting majors who all want my position at The University of Arizona. I have worked with students who have had little to no hand/eye co-ordination to those for whom the gesture was quite natural; students who were petrified to be "in charge," to those for whom the spotlight was a comfortable place to be. From this diverse group of students there is one concept that they have all needed: "Less is more!" In other words, make the conducting express the meaning of the music.

For these long years I have struggled to find the tools that would help all conductors, myself included, make the connection between gesture and sound, thereby becoming an "informed and informing mover." Ultimately, conductors must find a connection between their understanding of the musical score (the intent) and their action (the conducting gesture). For many students of conducting, an insufficient personal body awareness can hinder this connectivity. This old dog thought he had explored it all until now—but not any longer! Lisa Billingham's thoughtful and concise investigation of and prescription for the movement process of conducting via the body awareness methods of Rudolf Laban and the fundamentals of Imgard Bartenieff provides the "kinesthetic toolbox" to enable conductors at all levels to attain a technique that will foster meaning-making on the podium. Most helpful are Billingham's own methods, exercises, and applications of the Six Patterns of Total Body Connectivity that speak directly to the fundamentals of expressive conducting.

Who needs yet one more textbook about conducting? Only those conductors, teachers of conducting, and us old dogs who breathe and gesture need this one.

Bruce Chamberlain, DMus
Professor of Music
Director of Choral Activities
The University of Arizona

Acknowledgments

My inspiring teachers in chronological order: Eph Ehly; James Jordan, who gave me my first introduction to the concept of Effort at a conducting class at Westminster Choir College; and Maurice Skones, Josef Knott, and Bruce Chamberlain, my mentors at the University of Arizona and witnessed my first experimentation with Laban during my doctoral studies. My conducting colleagues at The University of Arizona survived my first gesture study with Laban and gave wonderful feedback and support during my lecture recital. Nicole Lamartine and I took our first Laban class together and have both grown to love and live Laban in our professional and personal lives.

The Integrated Movement Studies faculty with whom I received my training will forever be remembered as the most treasured individuals in my study of Laban training: Janice Meaden, my first teacher during my doctoral studies, Peggy Hackney, the project leader during my Certification, Ed Groff, and Pam Schick. Thank you for allowing a musician to move in a room full of professional dancers! To my IMS classmates, you will forever be my BESS colleagues. Thank you to Jodi James for the Labanotation sketch in Chapter One.

The members of the George Mason University Chorale and my conducting and graduate students, all who have been subject to many years of experimentation with gesture, rehearsal strategy, and conducting study sampling: you are my musical family, and without your music-making, this book would have no home. Of special note are the students who helped with my IMS Certification Project: Kristen Crocker, Chantel Pomerville, Jaime Schermer, and Christina Swett.

Above all, I'd like to thank my supportive family: my parents, Dr. William E. and Shirley Billingham, and my sisters, Gail, Jane, and Page for putting up with the thousands of hours I spent playing on the piano as a child learning my art and traveling the world to study. To my new family, I thank Diane Leader for the early edits on this book, Kevin Alvey for designing the fonts, and Jay Schober for his love and support through the entire process of Certification and authorship. You are my soulmate.

I would like to extend a final thank you to Alec Harris for believing in my research and Gregg Sewell for editing the book.

Introduction

As humans, we are movers. Each movement through intent sends a signal to the environment and those around us. These signals are important in the overall structure of a personal movement signature. The interpretation of our movement signature can greatly affect how we are perceived as conductors. Learning how to identify and create these messages is fundamental to conducting and leading a successful rehearsal.

As individuals, we have habitual gestures and body postures that define us in the environment, and over time we learn to rely on these as signals for non-verbal communication. This ability allows for a quickly paced rehearsal, as a posture in combination with a conducting gesture can communicate acceptance or displeasure at a moment's notice. *The Complete Conductor's Guide to Laban Movement Theory* explores strategies for the meaning-making process of conducting through a series of patterns. These patterns in the body and the environment around us create comfort in establishing a relationship between singer and conductor.

The capacity to lead an ensemble through the meaning-making process at any level requires the body to be balanced, strong, and connected. This sense of connectivity is created by the relationship of body movements to the core. Connection in movement fundamentals requires that the body movements are mindful and sensate.

Young conductors are often encouraged to learn beat patterns and releases as a means of introduction to the gestural language. It is my contention that conducting students should engage in exercises of body awareness prior to initiating the practice of gestural language. "Sensate knowing," or body knowledge, is essential to a healthy, connected, and vibrant conducting persona.

Howard Gardner's *Frames of Mind: The Theory of Multiple Intelligences* identifies natural patterns of learning styles in students. This is very important when working with conductors, as the skills require a knowledge base of kinesthetic patterns and abilities. Not all conducting students have developed kinesthetic intelligence, but I believe that body awareness can change the level of kinesthetic ability in the conductor.

Body awareness can be practiced in numerous ways through simple explorations of movement in connection to breath patterning. Breath is the source of life for our beings, and conductors who practice daily breath work, either through meditation or awareness exercises, will find a sustainable reservoir of energy for rehearsal and preparation for practice. *The Complete Conductor's Guide to Laban Movement Theory* provides exercises in various developmental stages of the movement process and gives suggestions for personal exploration of body awareness. It is this body awareness that gives a structure for success as an *informed mover*.

Philosophically, I believe that integrating the art of conducting includes movement from a physical, emotional, intellectual, and spiritual level. As an informed mover I can make decisions about how to move my body from a physical standpoint; a kinesthetic way of knowing. Emotionally, conductors will sense and interpret what needs must be met to inspire the choir to change its sound and respond in the rehearsal setting. Musical decisions must be met to create the sound desired as called for by an interpretation of the musical score. This intellectual ability can be aided by the Effort Life the spirit must exhibit to be connected to the choir with stylistic intent. It is the *combination* of these components that makes for a connected conductor.

The phrase "informed mover" is coined for a very specific purpose. Individuals who embody Laban have freshly informed intellectual ways of knowing how to best energize and activate connections in the body as they move. It is important to state that the spirit must be willing as well, to lead the mind and the body when they have come to a point of confusion. Many educators define confusion as a state of learning. This adage promotes the idea that processing new information requires a period of adjustment for new behaviors and patterns to be accepted. *The Complete Conductor's Guide to Laban Movement Theory* provides leadership for such a change. In order to move as a totally connected individual, parts must function in isolation and be connected to re-pattern the body into a more reliable, congruent mechanism for movement and expression. Newly developed tools and connections in the body, mind, and spirit will bring heightened capacity as an informed mover.

The ability to express music on an artistic level is possible for beginning and advanced conductors. The realm of possibility for expressive movement is often contained in how one learns conducting fundamentals such as posture, patterns, and release techniques. There is a necessity for conductors to explore basic movement skills. Identification of the body core from which humans move on an operational level is basic to movement. Exploring the potential for expressive and meaningful movement supported by the core is the main premise of this text.

WHY LABAN?

Laban Movement Theory explores the whole body as an entity that interacts with and has an impact on the environment in which it lives. Many of the other movement theories I explored for advanced study in relationship to teaching/conducting were based on movement in very specific terms that related to movement from a part of the body, not treating the body as a whole. There was also very little consideration of the psychological impetus for initiating movement with a purpose in these theories. We, by nature, are expressive in our daily lives in conversation and therefore have the capacity to add that personal dynamic to the rehearsal setting and conducting gestures themselves.

As a young conductor, I often found my gesture basic and the result from my choir very "vanilla." Understandably, there are times when this tone color is appropriate for literature, but alas, all of my literature sounded the same in rehearsal and performance. I yearned for a way to be more expressive and find a way to create specific gestures for use every day in the classroom.

Laban Movement Theory has been that vehicle for my teaching on the podium and developing a more dynamic and fulfilling life. Through training and research, I now have a variety of ways to draw unique tone colors and design a rehearsal that is exuberant and focused. I have learned to observe others and understand the internal motivation that is being demonstrated in an outward fashion. Experiencing Laban training has changed the dynamics of how I interact with my ensemble, and it gives me the ability to understand what dynamic energy my ensemble members are using to participate in performance.

The Complete Conductor's Guide to Laban Movement Theory provides a kinesthetic toolbox of exercises, which are ways for conductors to explore movement within parameters of theoretical practice from a physical and intellectual perspective. The joy of movement in conducting stems from the reality that, when moving to elicit a predicted and habitual response from an ensemble, the body is representing the sound it wants to hear. Building this vocabulary with the body gives a conductor a palette of options for functional and expressive results.

Chapter 1 is a brief history of Laban, introducing him as a theorist and his myriad talents as a dancer, choreographer, and artist.

Chapter 2 presents Bartenieff Fundamentals, a series of practical movement exercises for the body. These are based on basic neuromuscular patterns that remind the body of ways to move in an integrated and simple fashion. Body Connectivity is a fundamental component to healthy conducting. The human body can be re-patterned and re-minded of the potential for enlivening and connecting movement from a body core perspective.

Chapter 3 provides a tool for creative movement with intent for stylistic artistry. It contains numerous suggestions for self-discovery and intent for what conductors can use to make movement expressive while conducting. A vocabulary for specific stylistic gestures is included.

Chapter 4 presents a process for exploring Space, the body Kinesphere, and how the body's potential for creative expression is housed in the sharing and integration of body/mind/spirit. Physical delineations of the planes of the body and approaches to the environment are labeled in order to codify our place in the world as conductors.

Chapter 5 deals with the characteristics that describe our body movement potential and labels for stylistic identification and clarity. As humans we have natural affinities and tendencies for a movement palate that identify us as individuals. Changing the form of the body changes the intent of the movement.

Chapter 6 addresses modalities of application to make movement meaningful in relation to conducting and musical expression. Systematic patterning of individual movement signatures gives conductors a means of practicing expression through Laban Movement Analysis.

Chapter 1
History

Rudolf Laban (1879–1958) spent the majority of his life observing styles of human movement. As a child, he traveled extensively with his father, an Austro-Hungarian military officer, and, according to one author, "became interested in the movement profile of various cultures, including the American Indians, the natives of Africa, peoples of the Near East and the Chinese."[1] It was not only dance that inspired Laban to observe human movement; his fascination grew from exposure to numerous rituals in his travels throughout Europe. Observations of military ceremonial displays through movement in musters, parades, and funerals also interested the young Laban, and the observation of dervish dancing,[2] practiced as a precursor to battle, especially intrigued him.

As a physical outlet in preparation for an incumbent combat, Dervish dancers would often get into a state in which they could drive needles and nails through their cheeks, chest, and arms without suffering blood-loss or pain. These states of prayer were created not through physical movement alone, but by the addition of a focused mental state. The extended movements were both out of control and intense. "It is impossible of course, to describe the essence of the movements. But sometimes one can experience the same sort of tremendous impulse to move, for example, in a fight, in danger, in ecstasy, and in passion; in short, in times of excessive emotion."[3]

These early experiences convinced Laban that experimentation with combined movements could create inspiring and life-long challenges through the marriage of a mystical state and the physical pushing of the body to its limits. "The thought of the magic in dance held fast in my mind, and my decision to give my life to the arts became irrevocable."[4] Laban later created his scales work in relation to these patterns which he observed in his youth.

As a student, Laban went to Munich in 1900 and subsequently Paris to study art and architecture, but he was soon uninspired by studying these arts in isolation. Laban's father expected him to follow in his footsteps as a military officer, but he attended only one year of military academy. Laban received a small stipend and a letter of introduction to society in Munich from his father. To support himself, he took odd jobs as a sketch artist, actor, and coordinator for small revue shows. This exposure, together with his earlier studies in architecture, was the genesis for Laban to create a dance theater in Paris. Inspired, he designed his ultimate performance space, a theater in the round for dancers.

Laban settled in Munich in 1908 and lived there through 1914, designing movement activities and festivals while there. Beginning in 1910, he developed the concept of the *movement choir* and promoted it throughout Germany. Movement choirs are *not* singing ensembles; they are a group of movers with a common intent. These choirs consisted of a large body of people with various levels of training ranging from professional dancers to amateurs. Laban choreographed and led dance movements for the professional dancers and invited the amateurs to draw from the repetitive movements they performed at work (industrial or otherwise) to create a *movement choir*. The focus on these blocks of individuals was to "play" and create an experience in the joy of shared movement. Early movement choirs were based on movements given to groups of people at three height levels, high, medium and low, to create a three-dimensional representation of the group dynamic happening at the time. Movement choirs traditionally have a leader who assists with the coordination of the choreography created from the theme of the movement. A community building a movement choir might do so on a theme of joy, celebration, or any message they want to share through an expressive moving experience.

Laban's first school, established in 1910, was a place for dancers to further liberate themselves from the limited pairing of music and dance. Students were encouraged to explore movement in a less-confining environment with classes outdoors, free from the walls of a studio. From 1911–1914, workshops, schools, and performances were held in Munich in the winters and in Ascona, Switzerland in the summers. The festivals he coordinated in Ascona continued his work with movement choirs, and observers of these festival performances were often invited to join as participants.

Improvisation by his students led to Laban's groundbreaking concepts of the spatial harmonies of dance. Laban believed that studying movement within a framework isolated from the confines of musical structure allowed for new freedom of expressivity in movement. This new freedom led to an expression in dance that was formed solely by the rhythm of bodily movement and its spatial and dynamic components.

Mary Wigman, a student of Jacques-Dalcroze, who later became one of Laban's most famous students, integrated his early explorations with his concepts of drumming accompaniment, musical harmony, set design, costumes, and the spoken word.

Laban remained in Zürich during World War I and began his manuscript for *Die Welt des Tänzers* (*The Dancer's World*), which was published in 1920. This described Laban's belief in the uniformity of human movement patterns, particularly those of dancers. This text was developmental; Laban realized less than ten years later that some of the ideas in *Die Welt des Tänzers* were incomplete. Laban's level of creative drive and development at this time in his career made *Die Welt des Tänzers* a good place to start, but not the definitive book on Laban Movement Theory.

Laban's work was soon recognized throughout Europe, and he received invitations to choreograph productions. "Laban was called to the National Theatre in Mannheim to re-establish ballet and movement by the presentation of his own productions."[5] Dance schools in Europe were being run by Laban's students, and his reputation flourished. His Choreographic Institute was moved from Würzburg to Berlin in 1926; and in 1929, he directed a movement choir of 500 participants for a Mannheim festival. Concurrently, Laban relocated his school from Berlin to the

Volkswageschule in Essen, a center for the study of all art forms; dancers Kurt Jooss and Sigrid Leeder were involved in the dance department at the Volkswageschule. It was here that certification and testing for all students of Laban's Movement Theory began, with Laban administering the rigorous examinations himself. He returned to Berlin in 1930 to assume the directorship of the Allied State Theatres. However, Laban was soon to experience the first barriers to his ideas, fueled by the changing political climate in Europe.

Laban had been offered (and renewed) several six-month contracts as the Director of the Deutsche Tanzbühne beginning in 1934; in 1935, he published *Ein Leben für den Tanz* (*A Life for Dance*). His main responsibilities as director were to choreograph and organize performances of German dance. He reported to Joseph Goebbels, Hitler's propaganda minister tasked with transforming all arts to conform to Nazi ideals. Though Goebbels' main focus was the press and radio, as one of Hitler's top aides he was required to promote dancers in roles according to Hitler's vision, which labeled men as only folk dancers. Thus Laban's integration of men and women as equals in the movement choir was fatally damaged, making his creation obsolete in Germany. It was not until after he left Nazi Germany that Laban was able to further develop his movement theories.

In spite of the limitations on his artistic growth, 1936 was a pivotal year for Laban in Germany. He had become a German citizen in 1935, and was given several major responsibilities during the 1936 Olympics—choreographing and coordinating the opening performance of the Olympics and the sponsorship of an International Dance Competition. Laban was obliged to do as Hitler commanded, since to ignore Nazi directives would result in serious consequences.[6] The dress rehearsal of *Tauwind*, the prologue to the opening ceremony, brought disaster. *Tauwind* was based on the premise of "harmony between man and nature" (Hackney 1995). Music from Beethoven's Ninth Symphony was chosen to accompany the choreography, but it had to be replaced with a work by Hans Claus Langer, as the Beethoven was being used in the opening ceremony. The audience in the open-air theater was amazed by the performance. Hitler and Goebbels attended, yet did not share the audience's enthusiasm, as the dance promoted equality of both sexes. An entry in Goebbels diary the following day reads:

> Rehearsal of dance work; freely based on Nietzsche, a bad, contrived and affected piece. I forbid a great deal. It is so intellectual. I do not like it. That is because it is dressed up in our clothes and has nothing whatever to do with us.[7]

Goebbels cancelled the performance of *Tauwind* and executed a mechanism by which all publicity regarding the performance was halted.

Laban was dismissed from the 1936 Olympics, and the authorities searched for ways to banish him. His ties to freemasonry were used to justify his dismissal, and Laban received notification that all Freemasons were considered outcasts. "Laban and all those associated with him were now in mortal danger."[8] Laban received a last-minute invitation from the French Ministry for Foreign Affairs to present a lecture at the International Congress on Aesthetics in Paris in 1937 and seized the opportunity to flee Germany.

Three of Laban's students, Kurt Jooss, Sigrid Leeder, and Lisa Ullman, had established a school in Dartington Hall, England; he was invited to join them in 1938. Because of his German citizenship, he was allowed in England as a guest lecturer, but was unable to work as a teacher in an official position.[9] He gave unofficial lectures that Lisa Ullman arranged for him and lived in constant fear of deportation. Word of his work spread, and to relieve any tensions with the government, he would sometimes allow Ullman to give lectures on his behalf. Later in life he was regarded as a scholar, and was allowed to give open lectures, but during this time, he was dependent on others for mobility and relied on word of mouth to promote his work.

Finally, Laban was able to offer a series of movement courses for teachers from 1940–1946, and in 1946 Laban made the final move of his life to Manchester. Ullman had opened the Art of Movement Studio, which later became the center for educational dance in England. Laban's book *Modern Educational Dance* was created in 1948 through his work in Ullman's studio.

F. C. Lawrence, an industrialist, invited Laban to apply his movement notation and theory to industry, analyzing worker motion efficiency in factory situations in London. He was asked to document worker motions, so that industrial work could be adapted to work that was more productive.[10] His experiences with Lawrence led to *Effort* (1947), a source for successful industrial movement on which Lawrence and Laban collaborated. The success of the Lawrence/Laban collaboration resulted in Laban's theories being expanded even further. Another colleague and student, Warren Lamb, was instrumental in exploring the application of movement analysis to the field of psychiatry. Later in life, Laban Movement Analysis (known as LMA) was applied to work in various fields in England and abroad.

Laban's desire to define personal identity and expression through movement is still active today. His work was known in Europe, but through the efforts of two of Laban's students (Irmgard Bartenieff and Anne Hutchinson), his work was continued in Effort/Shape and Labanotation in the United States.

To this day, The Dance Notation Bureau at The Ohio State University and the Laban Institute of Movement Studies (LIMS) in New York are two of the more well-known institutes for Laban training in the United States. Integrated Movement Studies faculty Peggy Hackney, Janice Meaden, Ed Groff, and Pam Schick offer a certification program for Laban Movement Analysts on the west coast of the United States. The Laban Centre for Movement and Dance (formerly The Laban Art Center) in England was established as an educational trust for the public to access Laban's collection of charts, manuscripts, and models, and is a source for Laban's writings and sketches.

LABANOTATION

Notation was a vital part of Laban's efforts to establish an accurate descriptor of his movement system. Movement, to Laban, was a series of motions that a body passed through; there were no set positions, but a progression of movement *through* movement. Laban focused on devising a notational system that would depict the notation of *motions*, not positions (as could be done with traditional dance).

Laban spent the first half of his career designing his notational system. Its development flourished in 1926 with the assistance of several of his students, Sigrid Leeder, Kurt Jooss, Dussia Bereska, and Albrecht Knust,[11] who assisted Laban in handling concerns that came from their individual perspectives as graphic artist, musician, dancer, and notator, respectively. A major concern for the final notation system was the proportion of timing. Laban devised signs that would encompass movement in three-dimensional terminology.

> Each sign was like a letter, which clustered together to make "words"; but the flow of movement was not amenable to this mode of analysis. It was Jooss, apparently, who suggested that they should try opening out the matrix from a cross with four spaces for signs, to lines with four columns for signs.[12]

These columns were easy to pair with a musical score, enabling the brevity or elongation of a movement in proportionate time with the printed music. On the next page is an example of Labonotation of someone getting out of be in the morning.

Laban was encouraged to publish his system, as were other choreographers at the time. It was difficult for Laban to choose an appropriate label for his system. According to one biographer, "It was a *Bewegungsschrift*, a script of movement, but the name *Kinetographie* was decided upon to distinguish it from Feuillet's eighteenth-century *choréographie*. The profession of dance notator was a new concept and written dance the new domain."[13] It was apparent that Laban had studied, or at the very least been exposed to, Feuillet's *choréographie* in Paris, but the unique factors Laban included (describing movement through to the next movement) isolated his Kinetographie system from prior choreographic notation.

American Specialists in *Kinetographie Laban* were later trained by Anne Hutchinson, a student of Laban during his United Kingdom days who brought his ideas to the United States in the 1930s.[14] She eventually coined the phrase *Labanotation* to describe his notation system. Although Laban was not fond of this label, he did agree to it for some of his work in industry. Laban was aware that his work would eventually be adapted by others. He realized that dancer and notator Albrecht Knust, who was the *Kinetographie Laban* specialist in Europe, was often in disagreement with the changes Hutchinson had made[15] to Laban Movement Theory notation (or *Kinetographie Laban*). Hutchinson eventually created a textbook on *Labanotation* that is frequently used by the Laban Institute in New York and by other Laban teachers as a resource for understanding Laban's system.

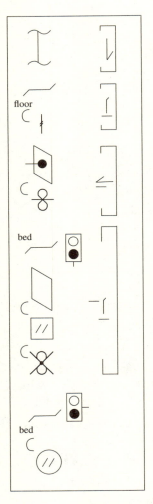

Walking

Standing

Upper-lower pattern rotating quarter turn (as though sitting at the edge of a bed)

Stretching with core distal into a square shape, rotating to left so back is supported by bed

Lying in Ball shape on right side of bed

FIGURE 1.1 GETTING UP IN THE MORNING

CHAPTER 2
BODY

> Bartenieff Fundamentals is an approach to basic body training that deals with patterning connections in the body according to principles of efficient movement functioning within a context which encourages personal expression and full psychophysical involvement.[16]

Irmgard Bartenieff (1900–1980), a dancer and student of Laban in Germany in 1925, immigrated to the United States in the late 1930s. After training as a licensed physical therapist, she developed the area of "Body" in Laban's theory and founded the first training program in New York in 1965. This later became the Laban Bartenieff Institute for Movement Studies (LIMS).

Bartenieff Fundamentals, as they are now called, are a series of movement patterns and exercises that Bartenieff developed with her physical therapy and dance therapy clients. In *Body Movement: Coping with the Environment*, co-authored with dancer Dori Lewis, Bartenieff describes the Laban Movement Analysis now used by Certified Laban Movement Analysts (CLMA). In the Appendix, she promotes her Fundamentals, expounding on the twelve basic exercises of her philosophy. This theory differs from other philosophies of movement and movement therapy in that the final goal is the interplay between the actions of the body and the intent of the action to create connected movement. Building a connection from the intent, through the action, to the outcome can be a difficult task if there are hindering qualities in body connectivity. In order to give a choir an indication of what is needed stylistically for a piece, the conductor has an expectation that is inwardly desired and outwardly expressed with the body through vocal commands and the conducting gesture. The conducting gesture should match the inner intent. This is achieved by body awareness and the freedom to creatively dance and play with the music being conducted.

This chapter explores the Six Patterns of Total Body Connectivity and how their application can develop a movement sequence to enhance conducting skill and expression. Interspersed with the text are some methods I have used as a choral conductor that I hope will serve as helpful examples.

The Six Patterns of Total Body Connectivity include Breath, Core-Distal Connectivity, Head-Tail Connectivity, Upper-Lower Connectivity, Body-Half Connectivity and Cross-Lateral Connectivity. These developmental patterns are supported through body connections that can be exercised for body awareness and aliveness.

The Six Patterns of Total Body Connectivity are in parallel relationship to infant patterning as studied by Bonnie Bainbridge-Cohen in her Body-Mind Centering work.

As the infant develops, Cohen's work compares developmental movement to human infant development (known as ontogenetic) and the natural progression of creatures in the animal kingdom (phyrogenetic). Cohen labels Basic Neurological Patterns based on ontogenetic and phyrogenetic development, and she claims that all developmental patterns must be experienced in order for humans to reach their maximum movement potential. If the patterns are not experienced in the first few years of life, the body has the capacity to adapt by traveling the pathways as an adult.

Peggy Hackney, a Bartenieff student, expands on Cohen's and Bartenieff's concepts and work in *Total Body Integration Through Bartenieff Fundamentals*,[17] which presents detailed descriptions of movement patterns and the application of movement patterns for a connected body. Hackney's Patterns of Total Body Connectivity (PTBC) create a stable baseline for exploration. Through a combination of physical exercises and body awareness techniques, adults can use PTBC to revisit and, if necessary, re-pattern the body for a more complete palate of movement potential.

Patterns of Total Body Connectivity (Peggy Hackney) Adult labels	Body-Mind Centering (Bonnie Bainbridge-Cohen) Infant development	Phyrogenic Development Relationship to animal kingdom	Symbols
Breath	Cellular breathing/respiration	Respiration of all cells in the body	
Core-Distal Connectivity	Navel radiation	Starfish—initiation of movement is from the core out to each limb	
Head-Tail Connectivity	Spinal movement	Fish—initiation of movement from the spine	
Upper-Lower Connectivity	Homologous movement	Frog—initiating movement from front or back limbs	
Body-Half Connectivity	Homolateral movement	Reptile—initiating movement from paired left or right side limbs in tandem	
Cross-Lateral Connectivity	Contralateral movement	Horse—initiating movement with left front limb and right back in oppositional response to pairing right front limb and left back limb	

TABLE 2.1 PATTERNS OF TOTAL BODY CONNECTIVITY

Practicing PTBC can be explored in various ways to best serve the movement signature of the mover. All patterns can be practiced on the floor, seated in a chair, or standing. An important factor to consider is that the patterns, once learned, can also be practiced out of order, so long as the recognition of all patterns is made from a place of kinesthetic knowing.

The PTBC exercises give extensive physiological descriptions of all six patterns. Developmental patterning has an underlying level of support from one pattern to the next: Breath supports all of the patterns that follow it. As they progress, beginners can learn to identify a connection that may have been avoided or neglected in their movement development.

EXPERIENCING THE PATTERNS OF TOTAL BODY CONNECTIVITY

Take the time now to experience all six Patterns of Total Body Connectivity. Below are brief explanations of the terms, followed by ways to explore them from a seated position.

BREATH ∞

Breath, the most basic pattern, is related to respiration in the womb and cellular breathing. All of the cells in the body have respiration patterns that keep the body healthy and revitalized. Breath is a common thread among all humans. As we have anxious moments in life, we can sense a difference in breathing patterns, feeling the need to breathe faster or slower. Jagged breathing is often a sign of pain or apprehension. We are sympathetic to these patterns in others by observation and proximity; in times of crisis we are more apt to encourage others to "take a deep breath," as we know this can calm the body.

Meditation and breathing techniques are frequently prescribed by doctors to lessen the stress of our daily lives. Dr. Andrew Weil, the director of the Program in Integrative Medicine at The University of Arizona, has produced a series of meditations and breathing techniques that can be used to heighten body awareness by learning several breathing patterns. Exploration of these patterns can bring benefit to those who are training to be conductors.

Singers and wind players are aware of the diaphragmatic strength and breath capacity needed to sustain long musical lines. It is the expansion of the rib cage that allows the diaphragm to drop and therefore sustain a supported phrase. Following is an opportunity to explore your natural breath patterning.

Exercise

1. Find your balance by sitting with both feet flat on the floor in a relaxed position while softening the face and relaxing the jaw muscles.

2. Find your sitz bones (the lowest point at the base of the pelvic girdle) and be sure they are spread and supporting the torso.

3. Take one minute to observe your breath.

4. While sitting, close your eyes and simply take note of your breath and how it enters and exits your body. As in any meditation/body awareness practice, it is important to first simply notice your breath, not to force air in or out of the body.

5. Once you have established observation of your breath, become aware of what it might take to imagine that you can move your breath to other parts of your body. For example, take your dominant hand and place it on your chest.

6. Imagine that you are sending the impulse for your breath through your hand to enliven the chest area.

7. Choose another area on the body that you can reach comfortably and send the sense of energy from both hands to your knees.

8. Through this awareness practice you may find your mind wandering to other thoughts. As in any practice of this nature, simply return your mind to the purpose of the breath and continue.

9. Work to practice sitting for breath up to five minutes per day. This will give you a rest position to relieve stress and allow the body to restore a healthy balance of oxygen in the bloodstream.

In relation to conducting, the preparatory breath of initiation for the choir is fueled by the conductor. Having an awareness of your ability to prepare, acknowledge, and gauge your own breath patterning will prove useful in the sequential preparation for conducting practice and leadership. *Movement activation is preceded by the inhalation and exhalation of breath.* This practice will be applied to all exercises in this text unless otherwise noted. This is the opposite of breathing instruction for most workout regimens. The preparation and awareness of your own breath will bring life and vibrancy to your ensemble.

This exercise can be used to prepare the body for any movement, but is important prior to conducting. Breathing rates can affect the tempo of a piece if they are erratic or jagged.

Conducting Exercise

1. A breath ball is created by cupping both hands as if they were holding a softball. Rotation of the hands around an imaginary softball in the air is a way to activate and give a pulse to an ensemble as a warm up. A Hoberman Sphere (a science toy that contracts and expands) can also be used to represent the bulbous nature of the breathing mechanism.

2. With young singers I ask the group to put the breath ball in their hands and to move in Shape Flow (see the chapter on Shape) to establish group breath. This is activated by pulsing the hands as if they were holding the human heart.

3. Using this imagery with students gives them an additional sense of kinetic awareness that is supported by an image.

CORE-DISTAL PATTERNING

Core-Distal Patterning is the concept that neurologically, humans move from their core to their distal edges. There are six distal edges: two arms, two legs, and the two ends of the spine (head and tail). The emphasis in this pattern is to be sure that all six limbs can move in toward and out of the core. This can be achieved as a series of openings and closings in the body into and out of the core, which is the spinal center of the body. The body is organized to operate from the core as a central initiation, with all limbs of the body moving from this core. This becomes vital in the next pattern of total body connectivity.

Core-Distal Exercise

1. While seated, take time first to identify all six of your distal edges (arms, legs, head, tail), being sure to initiate all movement through the distal edges following a complete inhalation, moving as you complete the exhalation of breath. This will be consistent as each pattern layers onto another.

2. All movements in these exercises are connected to moving off the core; the core is the base for strength and support of movement.

3. An important thing to remember about Core-Distal Patterning is that it can be initiated from the distal edge or the core, but that the movement is connected *through* the center of the body to reach from one end to another.

4. Take the right leg and extend it forward, using the floor as a support to slide the limb out and retract.

5. Allow it to come back to a bent position as you are seated.

6. Repeat this pattern on the left side of the body.

7. Next, outstretch the right arm and then bring it back to the core of the body, realizing that there is a connection of the arm to the center of the body.

8. Repeat this pattern on the left side of the body.

9. The final two limbs that reach through the core are the head and tail. Take a moment to gently pivot the head from side to side. This brings awareness to the top edge of the spine.

10. *Never* **drop the head back as you practice this pattern, as you can pinch the nerves in the upper spinal area.**

11. Finally, take a moment to let your tail move in the base of the chair. You may find that your body is resistant to head and tail exploration if you have not previously activated this area.

Be patient with yourself as you begin these moments of body play. Once you have initiated movement into and out of core from all six limbs, you can play with the idea that the body can close into and open out of core. Imagine that you are a jellyfish that wants to take in food for digestion. Reach out from your distal edges to pull something to you and then close around it. When you are ready to open and explore for more food, consider moving from the core to again bring food to you.

Conducting Core-Distal Mirroring Exercise

1. This exercise is something that can be practiced with a choir, either seated or standing. Often I have used this method to help the choir realize that the head and tail have a function in activating the body for singing.

2. Ask the choir to stretch one limb out as they follow you in mirror fashion[18] and to consider moving with the exhalation of breath, not during inhalation.

3. Alternately aspirate the breath as an example so that they can hear the underlying breath that supports their Core-Distal Patterning.

Exercise

1. Conductors can utilize this pattern to promote a sense of whole body awareness. Young conductors often find that the moving arms or stable legs are sensed as separate entities tied to a single distal edge. Practicing the closing into core with all limbs reminds the body that it has a wider variety of movement potential that can be activated.

2. A creative use of this pattern is to actualize a beat pattern with all six limbs, one at a time. Placing a three-pattern in each distal edge will bring awareness to the level of movement potential that the body can create. This would not actually be used in a rehearsal situation, but the relational independence of hands and strength from the core will bring strength and creative mastery of the body to form.

3. The size of the pattern practiced is not the key issue, rather that the pattern can be activated in all limbs. It is crucial to allow the body playful experimentation with patterns outside of the textbook conducting box that is provided for pedagogical safety in controlling the size of conducting patterns.

4. Expressive play can be a good outlet for creative realization of body movement potential.

HEAD-TAIL PATTERNING

Head-Tail Patterning defines the body as an individual entity in the environment and establishes the body in space and within a personal Kinesphere.[19] This is important as the body begins to play a role in the environment that surrounds it. Head-Tail Patterning is based on movement from the spinal area from either end. The spine is considered the center of the body from a biological perspective.

Professional movers (dancers, actors, and singers) who learn to use the Head-Tail connection enhance their performance ability. This is perceived by others as heightened expressiveness in their movements. Western society is quick to deaden the pelvic area; being seated for the majority of a workday makes the pelvic area a place of support rather than movement. Culturally, the trend is to hide the pelvic basin in movement for activities other than dance performance.

Head-Tail Exercise

1. While seated on a Swiss ball or chair (Swiss ball is preferred for this exercise) with your legs balanced under your sitz bones, identify your tail (coccyx) in contact with the ball.

2. Rotate your pelvis forward and back to locate the base of the spine.

3. Next, take your dominant hand and place it on the top of your head.

4. With a light touch, tilt your head to the right and then left 45 degrees to feel the potential for movement.

5. **Remember: Do not attempt to tip the head backward in any of these exercises.**

6. The base of the back of the neck is the top of the spine. The spine is then connected to the skull. Midway between these points at the ear level is the AO Joint (Atlantal-Occipital). This joint can be identified from the outside of the body by the jaw hinge. Place one finger at each jaw point to indicate the AO joint. (This joint is used as a body balance point in the Alexander Technique of body movement.)

7. Imagine that you are a fish that can move from the head or tail through the air.

8. While seated, identify the tail and then the head distal edges, feeling free to move the body between these points.

9. Move from the tail with initiation and then from the head, creating an invisible line of connection through the center of the body.

10. Enlivening this pattern will bring a more expressive conductor to the podium as the body has more potential for movement through the body, rather than moving simply from the exterior edges.

UPPER-LOWER PATTERNING

Upper-Lower Patterning is a way to connect the upper body to the lower body in order to investigate the vertical "throughness" that must include grounding in order to support the body for conducting. The combination of grounding into the earth and reaching out into the environment allows the body to explore a wider range of motion. This also gives the body the opportunity to mobilize in all three planes (Vertical, Sagittal, and Horizontal). The planes will be discussed in detail in chapter 4.

This is an important pattern for conductors, as they need a strong connection to the earth to support the expressive upper body connection. The entire body expresses the inner intent of the phrase or meaning. To practice the connection of forming an expressive connection to the environment, one must have a pathway developed in the upper body.

Yield & Push is a concept that relates to the PTBC by supporting a Yield into the earth for strength to Push out into the environment. This is a critical concept for conductors and teachers to learn, as it gives physical and psychological strength to support individual creative ideas. Expressive ideas can have an outlet through the concept of Yield & Push.

Certified Laban Bartenieff Movement Analysts (CLMAs) are trained to isolate body patterning difficulties and then train individuals to find the connected pathways within the body. With a sense of inner connectivity, students are able to build a clear expression with the outer body. The following exercises present the opportunity to find a pattern of creative play between inner and outer connectivity.

The Complete Conductor's Guide to Laban Movement

Exercise: Seated Yield & Push

Yield

1. Begin seated in a chair. Face a wall with the palms of both hands at the diaphragm level touching the wall. Be close enough to the wall to have some flexibility in the elbows so that the arms are not extended straight out.

2. Using the floor for support, reach through both legs to support the body in a seated position. Imagine a cord tracing the inner side of both legs. This cord will allow you to Yield the weight of the lower body into the floor which is the basis for the concept of Yield.

3. The bending of the legs while seated allows activated femoral flexion. This is the capacity to bend the leg at the illiopsoas (crease between the leg and the pelvic area). This flexion then allows for extension of the leg out along the floor.

4. Support of the body is also identified by the strength of the tripod of the foot. The tripod is connected from the heel to the ball of the foot to the outer toe.

FIGURE 2.1 TRIPOD OF THE FOOT

Push

5. As the legs are supported by the earth, engage a Push into the wall with both hands, using the connection from the feet through the spine, across the scapula area and out both hands to push against the wall, connecting the body through the upper and lower portions of the body.

6. Be sure to engage the scapula area as a supporting mechanism and connection point from the arms to the tail. This connection is paired with the relationship of feet through the head.

7. Imagining the V-shaped relationship of these pairings will reinforce connections through the core and in relation to one another.

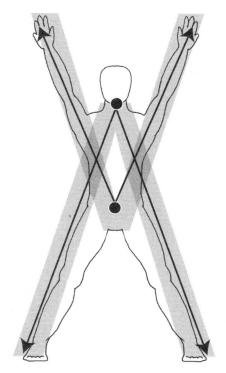

FIGURE 2.2 FEET TO HEAD AND ARMS TO TAIL CONNECTION

Upper-Lower Exercise
Partner exercise
1. Face one another and find your femoral flexion (Yield) as you stand one foot parallel to the other with the heels under the sitz bone area.
2. Connect your hands at the palm while the scapula drops to feel the connection from the arms to the tail. Your hands should be at the diaphragm level.
3. Match one another's pressure (Push), alternating in pushing one hand and then the other.
4. The mover receiving the Push is receiving by Yielding into his femoral flexion in the legs in connection to the earth.
5. Take turns alternating Yield & Push.

This is an excellent exercise for singers as well. This helps them to find the support of both feet into the earth. The legs can be parallel or one foot can be placed in front of the other. Many voice studios encourage singing posture with the dominant side forward.

GROUNDING

The Earth Provides Support, a Ground for Being and Moving. Human beings move in relationship to the earth and gravity.[20]

Grounding the body is a relationship to the earth. Humans create this relationship in order to move expressively and completely within their environment. Conductors understand that the body must be grounded in order for the limbs to move. However, the lower half of the body can be grounded for conducting without the body becoming tense or locked. As in all connected movement, grounding is forming a relationship to the earth that supports the weight of the body for intent. Body stability promotes effective mobility that supports creative and connected movement. The Theme of Stability-Mobility is a Principle of Bartenieff Fundamentals. "The sensation of being 'centered' or 'grounded' comes from being in touch with this center of weight area and its relationship with the center of the earth. This center is also a power source."[21]

BODY-HALF PATTERNING

> When highly articulated, differentiated movement is at issue, one cannot achieve greater mobility without first achieving greater support for stability.[22]

Body-Half Patterning is the organization of the body in halves divided vertically. One side is stable in order for the other side to be mobile. Consider placing a cap back on a tube of toothpaste. One hand holds the tube steady as the other screws on the cap. The dual action is done in a sided fashion, one side supporting the other. In Body-Half Patterning we also develop a sidedness of dominant support. The majority of humans are right-side dominant. Researchers suggest that up to thirty percent of humans are left-handed or ambidextrous. Note that as you are reading this text, the page-turning is designed for the right hand. Right hand dominance is related to a right-sided dominance in the body. As you consider your own body, ask yourself the following questions and mark a check in the appropriate box to the right:

	Left	Right
With which hand do I write?		
When I introduce myself to others, do I have a side of my body that I present forward to impress someone?		
If I drop something to the floor, with which hand will I reach to retrieve it?		
As I hug someone, which side of the body do I lean to have supported?		

TABLE 2.2 DOMINANT SIDEDNESS QUIZ

The answer to these questions will give you your dominant sidedness.

Hands have a prescribed function in conducting patterns. The right hand is assigned the beat pattern/pulse, while the left hand is used to give cues and make expressive gestures relating to phrasing, dynamics, and articulation. Within the right hand, some expression is present, yet there are limitations to how far out of the pattern a conductor may go.

Conducting with a keen awareness of Body-Half Patterning can articulate stability with the pattern hand to support mobility and independence in the expressive hand. Often independence of hands takes a great deal of time to master in conducting class. It is easy to mirror patterns with both hands; it is more taxing to channel two separate ideas.

Infants experience this pattern by Asymmetric Tonic Neck Reflex (ATNR)—alternating flexion and extension in one side of the body. As the infant wants to move forward on the stomach, he flexes one side of the body *in* and extends the other side *out* to reach forward and pull the body up. ATNR is indicated by a sidedness of the head leaning toward the hand side (which is extended) and then flexing the opposite side. As the sides change in opposition, the body moves forward on the floor. This concept of alternating movement with body halves can also be applied to the concept of Yield & Push as the body reaches forward to pull into the flexing side.

Exercise in Body-Half Imagery

1. While seated, imagine that one side of your body is made of Slinky® wire coils from the fingertips down through the toes. The opposite side is made of concrete.

2. Choose a side from which to move.

3. Which side did you assign as stable? Which as mobile? It would be easiest to assign mobility to the coil side as it has the ability to stretch.

4. Now imagine that the concrete side has magical powers that allow it to stretch like taffy and the coil side has rusted and can no longer move.

5. How has this changed your ability to move?

6. Imagine that whichever side you choose can be dominant. Would you always choose the mobile side?

Body-Half Exercise 1

1. While seated or standing, root the right side of the body to the ground and keep the arm of that side still and resting against the side of the body or on the knee for stability.

2. The left side is now free to be mobile and expressive.

3. Make a few gestures in the air with your left side distal edges to begin. Be sure to entertain any curiosity you might have with your feet. Gestures are not confined to the hand and arm.

4. Note how comfortable you are with keeping the right side of your body stable.

5. Switch sides and make the left side stable. Mobility has been restored to the right side of your body.

6. If you are right-handed, how does this serve you? If you are left-handed how does this serve you?

7. How might your answer be different from your fellow classmates?

Body-Half Exercise 2

1. Begin standing with your feet hip distance apart, balanced from your sitz bones through to your feet.

2. Balance the head from the AO joint (the joint that indicates the opening of the jaw) to support a buoyant spine.

3. Be sure to have a slight bend in the knees to encourage proper blood flow.

4. Place a conducting three-pattern in your right hand. This is assigned as your stable side.

5. Add a widening gesture in the left hand that sweeps the Horizontal plane expressively for one-three count (1–2–3) out and then one-three count in toward the center of the body.

6. Play with the speed and the pressure of the mobile/expressive hand. The important factor in this exercise is to promote stability on one side of the body.

7. Now that you have experienced the traditional application of stability and mobility in conducting, switch sides.

8. Begin with setting a three-pattern in the left hand.

9. Continue to establish this pattern until it is stable and secure.

10. When this has been accomplished, begin the creative and expressive right hand by exploring the Horizontal plane in a fashion similar to that used for the first half of the exercise.

11. Continue experimenting with movement in the other planes (Vertical, Sagittal) to experience the full realm of possibility for expressive movement in the right hand.

12. As you complete this exercise and can move between both hands in stability and mobility, what do you notice? Are you experiencing a new or heightened awareness of one side of your body? Does your Breath Patterning change as you switch sides? Can you still feel the underlying patterns of Upper-Lower and Head-Tail Connectivity?

13. Take a moment to record your answers or share with a conducting partner.

Cross-Lateral Patterning

Cross-Lateral Patterning is the most highly developed pattern. It relates to crawling in infants and animals that propel themselves forward with opposing limbs moving in tandem. Humans have a muscular and neurological relationship that crosses through the center of the body. This pattern can be traced on the body before it is activated.

Exercise: Tracing the Outer and Inner Connections

1. To trace this pattern, grasp lightly the outer three fingers of the left hand with the right hand, with the thumb on the top of the three fingers.

2. Release the hand and with the fingers trace up the outer part of the arm, cupping it to the scapula area. From the scapula the muscles are connected through the tail, behind the left leg and then traced on the outer edge of the right leg.

3. The tracing is completed once you have identified the outer three toes of the right leg.

4. Repeat this pattern using the left hand to trace the right outer musculature through the scapula area and down the outer edge of the left leg. This series has only identified half of the connection.

5. To trace the inner connection of the Cross-Lateral Connectivity, find the thumb and forefinger of the left hand. This time, you will trace a connection through the front of the body.

6. Gently grasp the thumb and forefinger with the right hand and trace along the inner portion of the arm (radius area) across the sternum and down to the belly core. The connection then travels through the lesser trochanter, over the illiopsoas and through the inner highway of the leg (inner right thigh) down the leg to plant and end at the first two toes of the right foot.

7. Take time to spread the toes and ground them to the earth before repeating on the other side.

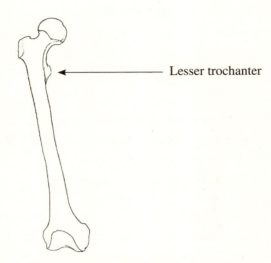

FIGURE 2.3   POSTERIOR FEMUR

8. Tracing the connections for Cross-Lateral Connectivity will bring awareness through sensation that the human body limbs support one another in opposition.

Cross-Lateral Exercise Closing in Opposing Limbs
1. While using one through-line for support from the chair and the earth (left leg to the earth and right arm relaxed), close the left elbow into the right knee, crossing over the body center.

2. Alternate this by grounding the right leg to the earth and closing the right arm into the left knee.

3. This is an exercise in connection and flexibility. The more you are able to stay grounded through your core as you connect opposing limbs, the stronger your support will be for easeful conducting.

4. Another way to practice Cross-Lateral Connectivity is to sit near a wall and initiate a Push from the left leg into the floor (grounding) and match that Push with the right hand against the wall.

5. Press the hand flat against the wall and sit close enough so that it is not a reach to touch it. The idea is not to push with force, but to realize how one side supports the other. The hand should be at the breathing/expansion level of the body.

6. As you match the wall with the hand, use your imagination to trace the inner and outer connections of the body. They are being reinforced by the support of your core.

Maximum movement potential is prepared by the active onset of Cross-Lateral Patterning. Conducting students may often find that the support of an expressive left hand gesture is activated by a refreshed sense of support from the right leg. This connection is the most difficult to achieve, but is by far the most rewarding in expressive capacity.

Cross-Lateral Patterning is significant in identifying conductors that have a healthy practice routine. Applying this pattern to conducting is pivotal. Conducting students must have the ability to stand for long periods of time while keeping the distal edges engaged in an expressive manner through Carving (see Modes of Shape Change) movements with the hands while maintaining a grounded core for stability in their breath. Awareness of these connections will bring more stability for heightened mobility.

CONCLUSION

Awareness of body patterning and the Patterns of Total Body Connectivity brings a heightened capacity for movement and movement strategy toward healthy conducting. Note that many of these patterns may be practiced without conducting, but that all six do have practical applications to a daily conducting routine.

The founders and developers of the Patterns of Total Body Connectivity encourage movers to practice one pattern at a time. Take the initiative to explore several ways to activate the inner connections that are fostered by these basic movement patterns. Should you identify one pattern that is more difficult, be patient with yourself and take time to play in that pattern.

Conducting is a very physical practice by nature that has the capacity for great expression. Vitality in conducting is reinforced with strong Breath Patterning as an underlying theme for movement. This is true for all movement, but in relation to the conducting art, it can support the ensemble with which you are working and prepare your own body for the task of expressive movement with meaning.

Exercise for All Six Patterns of Total Body Connectivity
1. As you become familiar with the aforementioned exercises, begin to pair and then perform all six patterns.

2. This may be practiced in any fashion you choose, but is most complementary to body awareness to explore in order from Breath to Cross-Lateral or the reverse, Cross-Lateral to Breath.

3. These are patterns that can be improvised upon once you can identify and feel the connection from distal edges to core.

Chapter 3
Effort

Human movement, with all its physical, emotional and mental implications, is the common denominator of the dynamic art of the theatre. Ideas and sentiments are expressed by the flow of movement, and become visible in gestures or audible in music and words.[23]

EFFORT

The concept of Effort is by far the most widely applied to areas outside the dance arena such as music and theatre. Effort is divided into four elements which delineate how we move in a dynamic fashion. The four Effort Elements are *Flow, Weight, Time,* and *Space,* and have numerous combinations within them that are activated in everyday movements. Combining Effort Elements gives us a unique movement signature that is often more recognizable by others that observe us in daily life.

EFFORT ELEMENTS

FLOW
Flow, an ever-present force, is our baseline ability to move. In relating this to movement we consider it a sense of "ongoingness" or constraint in

Laban training. Theoretically, once we initiate a movement, it continues forever until we stop it. Free Flow is a movement that has no end, and the spectrum reverses with Bound Flow. Imagine the onset of a balanced pendulum. Once the movement is started, the pendulum will swing forever. Initiating Bound Flow would be to reach out and stop the pendulum. We work and live in a constant "Flow Flux," balancing our movements to contain moments in motions that are contained and ever-moving.

WEIGHT ⊦

Weight is considered our ability to use the force of the body to exert ourselves and make a statement with our body presence. Society often uses the phrase "He really put his weight behind that idea." This is not relative to a person's individual weight; it is the personal strength one exhibits in a physical manifestation of a stance or opinion. Weight is either considered Light or Strong in Laban terminology.

Weight sensing (⊦) is in relation to my physical sense: my connection to the earth. It is about the inner awareness of how you are affecting your environment. Historically, weight-sensing was added to the Laban system when Twyla Tharpe's choreography came to fruition. This is much more about where you commit to the movement being made.

TIME _ ´_

Time relates to when a task needs to be completed. Time can be either Quick or Sustained. A task is in dire need of completion; it is a quick motion to grab a glass about to drop off a table, a sustained one when you are viewing a sunset over a long period of time to see a change in the hang of the sun over the horizon. As conductors it is important to note that Time does *not* relate to musical time/tempo.

Time also relates to the reinvestment of energy. We are dynamic beings that need to rest and restart motions in order for the nervous system to regulate and control our outward movement. Reinvesting our energy is a continual refreshment of our movement signature.

How does the Flow of the motion move?			
	Free Flow		streaming abandoned swinging a heavy object before throwing it
	Bound Flow		restrained holding back controlling the flow
How is the impact of the motion affected by Weight?			
	Light Weight		using a fine touch picking up crystal airy delicate
	Strong Weight		vigorous powerful smashing an object with a fist
When does the action need to be completed in Time? (This does not relate to the duration of a task.)			
	Sustained Time		leisurely taking time unhurried relaxed
	Quick Time		urgent hasty pressing
In what manner is Space approached?			
	Direct Space		demanding concentration pinpointing cueing one person
	Indirect Space		flexible encompassing focus cueing a section

TABLE 3.1 EFFORT ELEMENTS

SPACE ⌐

Space is interpreted in how we attend to our environment. Direct Space is to be fixed on a point; looking directly into a friend's eye, or focusing on one petal of a flower. Indirect Space is an ability to take in a great deal of a scene with no focus, as in walking into a party and meandering with the eyes and body to see what and who is in the room with no intent of selecting any one person.

EXERCISES:
EXPLORATION OF THE EFFORT ELEMENTS

The continuum of Effort is explored by isolating the Effort Elements for a brief period of time and then learning to combine them as you learn their labels. These Elements will aid you in labeling how your movement signature is designed and interpreted. Human movement is based on the combination of these Elements. Identifying your movement signature will be very important to explore as you work with ensembles. The ability to find, label, and change your movement signature style will have great value. The Effort Life that we convey to others seriously affects the sound of the ensembles with which we work. Flow, Weight, Time, and Space may be used in a myriad of combinations.

Here we will take time to explore each of these in isolation with the body, including the intent to fulfill these with clarity. Using your imagination and your body you may explore these Effort Elements in a chair, moving, or lying on the floor. The exploration of the following stories will bring you some indication of how you experience Effort: what comes easy to you and what might be a challenge to represent.

Flow ⌐

A. Imagine you are riding on the rushing Colorado River in a raft that does not stop. Focus on the feel of the raft as your body moves without any sense that it could stop. At this point, make your body the river that does not stop. As you will see, it is difficult to maintain Free Flow for a long period of time.

B. You are a small child in a park who sees an ice cream vendor across the walkway. You have permission to run as quickly as you can to the vendor. The path is not important. Run with abandon! As soon as you abruptly stop so you will not run into the cart, you have changed your flow from Free to Bound. The transition to Bound Flow is condensing the body to stop inertia.

Weight

A. You are a hummingbird that is about to light on a flower in midair. It is not important that your overall body weight is light, but that the gesture is a light action. This is an example of Light Weight.

B. It is winter and you have decided to chop wood for a warm fire. It will take your core brute strength to chop the log in half in order to cut the wood small enough for your fire. The strength with which you use your arm to swing through the log will require Strong Weight. In this instance, how physically strong you are is not important, as this is an exercise. The inner intent strength is what indicates Strong Weight, and how you use the weight of your arm.

Time

A. Imagine it is your day off. Your plan for the day includes reading the newspaper, stopping for a coffee, and perhaps stopping at the mall for the latest bestseller. These tasks can be completed at any time in any order, and there is no sense of expediency in getting any of these things accomplished. You are relaxed and completely unhurried. This is an example of Sustained Time. You might also wish to sit and lounge with your newspaper with no goal of completing the entire paper, or even reviewing the editorial section. These are actions that you wish to complete but do not need to be done in an expedient fashion.

B. You have a pot of water on the stove for tea and your child is sleeping in the adjacent room to the kitchen. The tea kettle whistles and you run to the kitchen to snap the kettle off the burner. This is Quick Time, and what is important to internalize is the idea of how quickly the *task* is being performed. You need to take a sip of water as a piece of bread you were chewing is causing you to choke. You reach for a glass vase after the cat chases it off a shelf.

The important element of Time is how quickly or slowly you reinvest your energy to take another action. It is more important to know that you could linger in the movement for Sustained Time and that Quick Time is about continually reinvesting your intent and movements.

Space ⊥

A. You are a first-time visitor to New York City. You are not aware of your own presence, but the multitude of large, shiny glass buildings that surround you in all directions. The awareness of too many things to observe or to focus on in numerous directions gives you the sense of Indirect Space.

B. Daydreamers often stare into an imaginary void where one idea or thought drives their attention. Although we will often say that we are staring into space, the mind has a thought that is pinpointed and very direct. When we focus our attention on one individual idea or one spot in space, we are experiencing Direct Space.

Imagine it is your first visit to the National Cathedral. You have stepped through the doors and see the tall ceilings. Using your Indirect Space, you notice not one individual attribute of the cathedral, but many things are in your focus: all the wonders of the cathedral. Although Indirect Space does not always have the intent of wonder, for this chapter, it may be easier to role-play using your imagination.

Pairing Direct Space and Psychological Kinesphere (dealt with in chapter 5) will give you a great physical presence and command on the conducting podium.

EFFORT ELEMENTS IN COMBINATION

Isolation of the Effort Elements of Flow, Weight, Time, and Space is not a simple task, as we typically move with these Elements in combination. Laban created his Effort Elements in Combination to give a vocabulary to label common motions that can be classified and notated within what he labeled States and Drives.

States combine two of the Effort Elements, while Drives combine three. These are more difficult to practice without detailed training, but it is important to note here that they do exist as a portion of Laban's theory. CMAs are trained in observation skills to identify how a person's movement is Effortful. This is particularly useful in how we work with evaluating others in their movement signatures. The most often applied combinations within the area of Laban Movement Theory are a series of actions that have been labeled within the Action Drive (-⊢). Action Drive has no Flow element. These are set as individual actions that happen once: set moments that can be easily identified.

Acting classes often insert these Elements to make a scene or statement more dramatic. Theoretically, it is impossible to sustain these short actions for any length of time (even though some are in Sustained Time). In consultation with my Laban mentor, Peggy Hackney, we discussed that moving through one Action Drive moment to another would require the insertion of Flow. To practice and activate these common Effort Elements in Combination they would need to be labeled as *Full Effort Actions*.

The concentration of body energy and mental focus of intent that it takes to complete these tasks includes Flow, as it is the baseline for all movement. Table 3.2 gives the Effort Action Movements from Action Drive. This is the one Drive within LMA that has labels for the motions. The table includes the Eight Effort Actions without the consideration of Flow. When you practice these movements, take moments between each action; any transition from one movement to another will require Flow and the other Effort Elements. One suggested motion for each Action is given as an example of a movement common enough to be recognized and actualized. Remember that there is an inner intent and an outward action within each of these Actions. If you do not have the intention to carry out the movement itself, the movement has no meaning. That is why you will see a brief description of each before you are asked to embody these movements in exercises.

EFFORT EXERCISE: EFFORT ACTIONS IN COMBINATION

Table 3.2 includes a description of the Effort Actions in Combination that can be used to practice building an Effortful Movement Vocabulary. As individuals, we are uniquely recognized in our movement signatures. The descriptions for the Effort Actions in Combination are only suggestions for the enactment of the Efforts. A blank box has been inserted in the table for a creative set of movements that you can create and write in the text or in a journal. Building a series of movements that have meaning for you individually is key.

Notice that each movement has intent. For example, in Slash (the removal of dishes from a table) the intent will help you use the requisite Strong Weight to clear all of the dishes. If you were to clear only one dish, the Spatial intent would be direct; the fact that you are covering a great deal of Space without a care makes the Space Indirect. The differences may be subtle in how they are applied. Review the Elements should an Action become difficult to perform so that you have something as an image for each of the Effort Actions in Combination.

CHAPTER 3 • EFFORT

TABLE 3.2 EFFORT ELEMENTS IN COMBINATION

EFFORT ACTION	FLOAT	PUNCH	GLIDE	SLASH	DAB	WRING	FLICK	PRESS
SYMBOL								
SPACE	Indirect	Direct	Direct	Indirect	Direct	Indirect	Indirect	Direct
WEIGHT	Light	Strong	Light	Strong	Light	Strong	Light	Strong
TIME	Sustained	Quick	Sustained	Quick	Quick	Sustained	Quick	Sustained
REAL LIFE ACTION	Pulling away from a hug while staring into space	Hitting a toy punching bag before it rebounds	Sliding your hands over a piece of silk fabric	Clearing a large table of multiple place settings with a dish towel	Tapping one drop of morning dew off a leaf of grass	Getting the water out of a wet piece of laundry by twisting	Removing lint off the shoulder of a jacket	Holding a ladder steady for support while someone is balancing on it
REAL LIFE ACTION CREATED								

39

EFFORT EXERCISE: EFFORT ACTIONS IN PAIRS

Take a moment now to experience the Effort Actions in opposite pairs. These will later be added to a series of movements in the cube. In the list below, find an image that you can use to perform each one of these individual Efforts. You may use your hands and body in the initial practice. Eventually you will want to isolate these movements into conducting gestures that you can practice and use as a system for style application to the score. It is important that you have an image from the beginning that relates to your movement signature so that you can bring these Efforts to life in application very quickly.

The opposites you will use for practice are:

1. Float/Punch
2. Glide/Slash
3. Dab/Wring
4. Flick/Press

Prior to practicing these opposites, have a description that works for your individual movement. Use the real-life actions you created and entered in Table 3.2 as suggestions for common movements that can get you started in the creative process. As you practice these pairs, speak the Action word you are displaying to pair the execution of the movement with your voice. Often as singers and conductors, we can relate the weight and timbre of our voice to match a description of a movement we are leading. For example, when experiencing the Light Weight in Glide (_⊢), you may find it easier to actualize if you add the inflection of your voice to match your Action.

Exercise: Using your Dramatic Voice in Conversation

In this exercise you will apply the Effort Elements in Combination to a conversation and then label/identify the Effort Actions that were present. Listed below are a series of short conversations that can be practiced in pairs or small groups. In a classroom setting of this exercise, it is best to split the speakers into small groups and then come back to the larger group for performance and labelling.

Be sure as you choose a situation that you have intent in mind for directing each line with emotion, and that you consider how you are using your body. Does a hand gesture help the situation? Will you be Direct or Indirect in your Space? Does that get the message across? Will you take your Time in how you deliver the message—and how does that affect the audience?

Situation A
Background

Student James: You are a student visiting a professor to contest a grade you received on a paper. It is your intent not to leave the office until the professor has agreed to your request. See what Effort Actions in Combination convey your request and ultimately give you the result you desire: a better grade.

Professor Smiley: A student is coming to your office to contest a grade on a paper. You have graded it very fairly and have no inclination to change the grade unless the student can convince you otherwise. You leave the meeting satisfied that you have graded the paper in a just fashion.

Dialogue

Student:	Professor Smiley, I am here today to ask about my grade on the latest paper that was due for your class.
Professor:	Miss James, What is your concern?
Student:	I believe my paper should receive a better grade.
Professor:	Your paper was graded quite fairly.
Student:	I am asking you to take another look at my paper.

Professor: Fine, please leave it in the office with me.

Student: Thank you.

Now that you have enacted this scene, ask your observers to label what Efforts came easily to you. Once you have labeled these, go back and take the following new intent into the dialogue.

Student: *You know that your paper deserves a higher grade, and if you go into the room with a modicum of respect and sincerity, Professor Smiley will change your grade.*

Professor: *Student James is always coming to ask for a grade change. Your mind is made up that you will not change the grade.*

Effort Observation
After this dialogue, how has your body changed to match your intent? Did you use more Direct Space? Did you reverse your use of Weight? Did you use shorter bursts of energy while delivering your lines? How did that affect the scene?

Situation B
Background

Scott: *You have made a new friend in Joan and want to ask her to go for a cup of coffee. You are very shy, but will take the chance to ask Joan, as you think you have things in common, having just met her on a hiking trip. You run into her in the grocery store after a long day at work.*

Joan: *You have recently moved to the area and want to make new friends. Scott was with you on a recent hiking trip, and you think he could be a new friend. You would like to spend more time getting to know him. You have gone to the grocery store to buy cat food. You are hoping that when you run into Scott, he will ask you to get together sometime.*

Dialogue

Joan: Hello. Didn't we meet at the hike last weekend?

Scott: Why yes, yes, we did.

Joan: I really enjoyed the changing color of the leaves, didn't you?

Scott: Yes, and the carpet they made on the trail.

Joan: I just stopped to buy some cat food.

Scott: Oh, you have a cat.

Joan: Are there good places to eat nearby?

Scott: Yes, and a nice coffee house.

Joan: Have you been recently?

Scott: No, would you like to go with me sometime?

Joan: Sure!

Effort Observation

What do you notice about your use of Effort in this scene? As Scott, did you use more Direct or Indirect Space? Did you rush to shake hands with Joan? As Joan, did you use your Effort Life to appear interested in Scott's conversation?

Now that you have tried this, change your intention in the conversation.

Scott: *You have met Joan, but are convinced she is too aloof to notice that you are interested in her. You are worried that Joan will reject your friendship, as she appeared not to notice you in the supermarket line ahead of her.*

Joan: *You caught Scott out of the corner of your eye as you entered the store. You would like to go with Scott for coffee, but you are in a hurry to get home and feed your cat.*

Observation

How did your Effort Life change as Scott? Did your shyness come through? As Joan, did you make your body convey the urgency of your trip for cat food? Was your answer "Sure" too short? Did you have a Dab in your hand as you accepted, or a Flick to indicate your Indirectness?

COMPLETE EFFORT ACTIONS AND THE CONDUCTING GESTURE

It is now time to explore the Complete Effort Actions with your conducting gesture. Using the pairs that you practiced in the previous exercise gives you the opportunity to add to your gesture and make the pattern dynamic! As you are moving between beats for the conducting gesture, there is the element of Flow as a factor. That is the reason we are now labeling these as Full Effort Actions. Using a basic two-pattern, add the dynamic intent of each of the Full Effort Actions to the downbeat of a continued set of two-patterns. Refer to the traditional two-beat conducting pattern in figure 3.1 below.

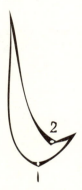

FIGURE 3.1 A TWO-BEAT CONDUCTING PATTERN

Do a preparation breath with each pairing. Once you have practiced and feel confident in all of your gestures, challenge yourself to add the Complete Effort Actions to a four-beat pattern. These should initially be practiced in pairs, with a transition of traveling with very even Flow between the pairs. This will give you the opportunity to prepare for the Complete Effort Action with your inner intent.

As you become more comfortable with the actualization of these individualized movements, you will be able to apply them confidently as a common part of your conducting movement signature. Take a moment to evaluate one another in class or find a partner with whom you may practice demonstrating your new gestural vocabulary. Explore and observe one another in what is most easy to actualize and what is most challenging. Discuss options of images and the inner intent you have in order to enact these gestures. You may find that a Complete Effort Action with Light Weight is more challenging to you, or that Indirect Space is difficult to do with Quick Time. Keep a journal of what Complete Effort Actions serve you as you begin to use them in your everyday life and conducting exploration.

CONCLUSION

The dynamism that can be added to the gesture with the Complete Effort Actions gives you a new range of expression. This new vocabulary that you are exploring will give a new breadth of sound to your ensemble. Explore these gestures with your ensemble to give a variance of color to the sound and a healthy warm tone.

There is no prescribed sound that will happen for an individual gesture, as we are all built differently. Strong Weight intent with someone of petite build may bring more dramatic changes to the sound of the choir, whereas a conductor with a long torso may use the same effort language and a lighter or different interpretation will result.

Overall, the purpose of training conductors in Effort is to bring dynamism to life in a range of characters. Conductors may often have a demeanor that is different on the podium than off. Practicing the range of what is possible gives the conducting student a new way of expressing how music is interpreted through the conducting gesture and the stature of the body. In the final chapter of this book we will explore how combining all of the elements of this system can deal in specific ways with the gesture and the score.

Chapter 4
Shape

Shape may be seen as pertaining to the body as a metaphoric "container" that is malleable and subject to forming the various body shapes.[24]

SHAPE

To express the idea of a harmonic series of patterns in nature and art, Laban referred back to the Greeks, who proposed that all elements in nature are in some form divisible within the circle. This perfect form is considered the "whole"; therefore, parts to the whole would exist within it. The Five Platonic Solids that have perfect roots within the circle are the Tetrahedron, Cube, Octahedron, Icosahedron and the Dodecahedron. Laban developed his Space Harmony Theory in relation to the proportion of "parts-to-whole," designing scales existing within these Greek Platonic Solids.

The term *scale* is used for the functional basis of proportions in art, music, and architecture. Scale has a proportionate relationship to the whole, and harmony creates a balance through scale design. Musicians understand the use and application of scales as a foundation for functional harmony in order to analyze and create music. The musical scale has traditional proportions of whole and half steps that create a functional and harmonic pattern. Similarly, Laban has created a series of scales to be performed with the body and within the Platonic Solids to create dynamic movement that is harmonic within the solid and in relationship to how the human body is constructed.[25]

Substantial work has been done by Warren Lamb (b. 1923) in continuing the work of Shape in Laban's Movement System. In *An Eye for Movement,* Dick McCaw describes Warren Lamb's career and interviews him on his work with Laban, citing portions of Lamb's journal work while he studied with Laban. Warren Lamb began his studies with Laban in 1946 in Manchester at the Art of Movement Studio, and he collaborated with F. C. Lawrence and Laban on Effort/Shape Analysis and training for factory workers. Laban encouraged his students and colleagues to use the facets of Lamb's work that applied to their work. Lamb's system of Movement Pattern Analysis is used today, and he actively teaches his adaptations. Two of his students are Irmgard Bartenieff and Judith Kestenberg, whose work we explored in chapter 2.

Ed Groff[26] describes Shape as the "physical form made visible by the constellation of body parts and the process of forming and transforming the body shape."[27] It is important to understand the difference between the process of form and "forming" the body. The Shape aspect of LMA is concerned with a) the form of the body, b) how the body is moving into a form, and c) the movement process that is taking place. These aspects of Shape will be explored in this chapter through exercises, self-exploration and observation.

OPENING AND CLOSING

The largest general element of Shape is Opening and Closing. This relates to the idea of flexion and extension, where the body is seen as recoiled and closed (flexion) and spread open wide (extension). As you are reading this book, you are either Open or Closed in your approach to the new material in your mind and about your body shape. The position of your body can explain to an observer how you are feeling about what you are taking in with your eyes. For example, you may be lying on the front of your torso, spread out on a bed with arms and legs splayed freely. This would be an Open body position.

Culturally, there can sometimes be dichotomy between a posture and its internal message. We say we are open to someone when we reach for a handshake or hug in greetings. However, such postures may sometimes be difficult to deny in situations where another person reaches out first. In that case, an astute observer may notice an acceptance of the gesture, but with a body message that is somehow turned away. When we see someone in a semi-fetal position, we would say that person is closed; attending to a need for self care. This may be the case if the person has just received bad news and wants time to reflect or feels threatened in some way. On the other hand, a closed body position can be a posture of celebration when a baby has just learned to roll over by closing the body, achieving movement across the floor.

Research has shown that being "closed off"—crossing our arms or legs to keep threats at bay—can be read as a negative attribute when interviewing for a job, meeting someone new, or being exposed to an unwelcome situation. In spite of such negative perceptions, these are useful times for being both Open and Closed. Opening and Closing creates a relationship between self and the environment. In a musical rehearsal, having the ability to move between these forms can bring respect, reflection, and response to your choir. The act of Opening and Closing—the "doing"—is critical in learning how to respond in a rehearsal situation so that all ensemble members feel equally able to share their thoughts and questions. Conductors need to find a balance in practicing Openings and Closings to create a sense of belonging for the members of their ensembles.

Opening and Closing Exercise
Part 1
1. Table 4.1 gives pairs of words that describe opposite Openings and Closings.

2. Take a moment to create a few word pairs of your own in the open boxes of the table. The words will be used with your conducting partner in a later exercise.

3. Note that the Openings and Closings have an active "ing" suffix as a part of the description.

OPENING	CLOSING
Exposing	Concealing
Releasing	Capturing
Greeting	Shunning
Accepting	Withdrawing

TABLE 4.1 OPENING AND CLOSING DESCRIPTORS

Part 2

1. Now that you have created a few pairings, practice embodying all the pairings with a partner in a short dialogue.

2. Create a situation where each person is one part of the pairing.

3. After you have practiced this, apply it to the podium. Practice a simple stance of Opening and Closing while you conduct a basic four-beat pattern.

4. Have a partner or a group of people in your class observe *how* you appear as you are Open and Closed.

5. Do you appear happy, engaging, desolate, detached? How might a simple change in posture affect the perceptions others read from you?

6. These exercises and observations will be addressed under Shape Flow below.

Observing Opening and Closing Exercise

It is time to practice observing the differences between Openings and Closings.

1. Below is a list of everyday life events. As you go through your day, log your observations by noting how *you* interpret whether the person is Open or Closed, and whether their Shape changed during the course of your involvement.

2. Notice how a tone in dialogue, eye contact, or body stance affects your response and possibly influences others.

    - Receiving change from a store cashier.
    - Meeting a friend for coffee.
    - Sharing weights/exercise machines at the gym.
    - Someone turning on (or off) the lights in a classroom/rehearsal room when others are in the room.
    - Interacting with someone playing a videogame on a computer.

3. After you observed these behaviors, what did you notice? Did someone remain Open when you thought they might shy away from you?

4. Did your observations fluctuate between observing someone as Open and Closed?

5. Was the body of someone Closed but the conversation Open?

6. How did that affect *your* response?

7. Keeping a journal of these observations over time will help you become aware of how you see others and how they may be interpreting your ideas and motivations.

SHAPE FORMS

The body creates basic shapes that can be labeled as the body itself is formed. These shape forms are used most often for observation of dance notation positions. Laban Movement Theory gives an explanation of how to notate when the body is shaped long: picture a competitive diver jumping into the water with arms outstretched above the body to form a Pin. A Wall is the body in a flat form with the arms and legs away from the body, similar to the Da Vinci drawing of the body. A Ball is defined as the body tucked into a ball. Screw is a curved position around the body core. The Tetrahedron is a shape of the body having several points in space, sharing the floor with a hand or foot for support. These are static forms that are easy to observe.

As you look at Table 4.2, consider where you might find these body shapes in people around you. For example, a soprano sitting tall in rehearsal but with crossed ankles may show a Pin for her upper torso but a Screw for her legs. A Broadway soloist at the end of a solo with his arms outstretched above his head could be displaying a Wall if the feet are apart. These are simple observations, and this is information for a fully-informed movement analyst, which you will become as you practice all elements of this theory.

SHAPE FORM	PHYSICAL DESCRIPTION	LABAN SYMBOL[28]
Pin	Elongated	
Wall	Flat	
Ball	Round	
Screw	Spiral/Twist	
Tetrahedron	Pyramid	

TABLE 4.2 SHAPE FORMS

MODES OF SHAPE CHANGE

The Modes of Shape Change involve *how* to change the body to form relationships. Changing your inner attitude can affect how you present yourself as your body changes within yourself or outward, toward the environment. As discussed in previous chapters, there is a relationship with all movement from an inner intent to an outward result. Peggy Hackney defines the Modes of Shape Change as "Your attitude toward changing the shape of your body in terms of whether the shape change is self-oriented or environment-oriented."[29] As we explore the Modes of Shape Change, be mindful that it is the *inner attitude* that affects the movement.

As humans, we relate to one another verbally and physically and have the capability to alter what we show outwardly to others. For example, when we have a secret and do not wish to divulge it to someone else, we may do something to change our body shape to keep the secret by closing off the body or not talking directly to someone. Learning to form relationships using Shape can help us to understand what our ensemble members may be telling us by posture and facial expression rather than by words or playing. There are three Modes of Shape Change: Shape Flow (⌣), Directional (⇢), and Carving (⌒).[30]

SHAPE FLOW ⌣

Shape Flow is identified by a movement that relates to the self. It can be as simple as changing a body joint to adjust a jacket so that it fits more comfortably by adjusting a shoulder or pulling on the sleeve. This is a simple motion that is not meant to change a relationship to the environment. Shape Flow awareness is helpful when adjusting the body before rehearsal for balance or to bring clarity to the mind for the purpose of rehearsal. It can also relate to observing your own breathing patterns before starting a new tempo on a piece. This settles your internal tempo, not a tempo for the ensemble. It is all about *you*.

DIRECTIONAL ⇢

Directional Shape Change has to do with the self bridging to the environment. The individual is moving in such a way that the body is becoming involved in the outside world. In earlier Laban training, Directional Mode of Shape Change was defined as Location-oriented Shape Change, meaning that there was a destination to the change. The Directional Mode of Shape Change gives you the ability to make a connection to the surrounding world, and these changes can be Arc- or Spoke-like. Arcing uses only one joint—moving your straightened forearm from the elbow, for example. The Spoke-like Directional Mode of Shape Change uses more than one joint. The mover is able to connect to the world around him. Spoking can be used as a way to analyze dry-beat conducting in recitative where there is a lack of movement through all three planes with the arm.

CARVING ⌒⌒⌒

Carving is the voluminous movement interaction with the environment. With Carving, the body has the ability to move three-dimensionally. You learn to adapt your movements in relationship to what is happening around you. Conductors use Carving as a way to change what they are hearing in rehearsal while performing. Carving is critical in conducting, because as we use three-dimensional forming of the arm. Psychologically, we are often Carving in motivating an ensemble. We have set a goal for rehearsal and have initiated the sound. How we move in relation to the sound we get back from the ensemble sets the tone for the ability to change.

> ### Exercise in Moving the Modes of Shape Change
> When moving in Modes of Shape Change, it is imperative that the inner intent is clear. You should know whether the intent is to change how you are relating to your environment.
>
> In Shape Flow—speak out loud—"It is all about me!" What does your breathing mean in relation to how you are moving? Are you thinking about moving as you read this exercise?

Do you change your breathing patterns when it involves the influence of others? As you consider this, you change your focus to include the environment around you.

Imagine that you are walking down a busy street full of people. As you manipulate your body around people, are you Carving in a three-dimensional way or simply Spoking with your arms to cut through the crowd?

Experiment with this in a group setting to observe one another, and your reactions and responses. The art of observation is an important skill to build as a teacher and conductor. You will learn many things about your students by observing how they move and communicate with you or in a group. No one way is prescribed.

SHAPE FLOW SUPPORT

Shape Flow Support is the process of internal shape change in the body. Shape Flow Support entails inner torso movement that can even be at the digestive level. When we move in even small amounts, it can change the way others see us.

As we move from a state of stability into Shaping—a process of forming into something new—we produce something that creates a reaction from others.

Conductors move to respond physically/externally to what they hear from the ensemble. Effective change creates a better tone, better posture, cleaner lines. In effect, "changing" our shape is a part of changing results. I find that adding even a small movement to a change in the abdomen allows the ensemble to breathe with more depth and have the ability to play for a longer amount of time. Rising (♭) in the mid-torso has affected the breathing capacity for my choir, which affects me as a conductor and conduit for sound.

SHAPE FLOW QUALITIES

When you add Shape Flow to movements outside the body in forming toward the environment, you are exhibiting Shape Flow Qualities. The movements relate to the Planes: Vertical, Horizontal, and Sagittal. These dimensions in space relate to which plane is creating the pull.

For example, Rising (↓) and Sinking (↑) ride along the Vertical Plane; Spreading (↓) and Enclosing (⸺), around the Horizontal Plane; and Advancing (⸺) and Retreating (⸺), in the Sagittal. Laban thought the most mobilizing order for practicing the planes for exploring maximum movement potential was in the order of Vertical, then Horizontal, and finally Sagittal. These can be practiced in a series of movements along the Planes with movements that can be small or large.

SHAPE QUALITIES	PLANE	RELATED MOVEMENTS OUTSIDE THE BODY
Rising ↓ and Sinking ↑	Vertical/ Steep	Reaching toward the sky Lowering to the floor
Spreading ↓ and Enclosing ⸺	Horizontal/ Flat	Opening the arms wide and feet apart Closing one side of the body over the other and crossing the legs
Advancing ⸺ and Retreating ⸺	Sagittal/ Suspended	Bringing the body forward and reaching an arm out Stepping back with the body and bringing the arm in toward the body

TABLE 4.3 SHAPE QUALITIES

Exercise: Shape Flow Qualities in the Dimensional Cross of Axes

All of these movements are in pairs along the Dimensional Cross of Axes.

1. Begin with the body in balance, arms resting at their sides, feet hip distance apart.

2. As you move along the Vertical Plane (⊥), take both arms and reach overhead, taking the heels off the floor to the highest point you can reach (Rising).

3. Now reverse this to bring the body closer to the floor and the arms down, relaxing the feet to support the body (Sinking).

4. Next, move along the Horizontal Plane (⊤), widening the body open with the arms outstretched on the Plane (Spreading), then crossing the right leg over the left and bringing the right side of the body Closed over the left (Enclosing).

5. The movement in the Sagittal Plane (⤢) is bringing the body forward with a step and widening the arms to embrace the space in front of you (Advancing).

6. Finally, step the body back and enclose the arms with the elbows around the torso (Retreating).

7. Practice these exercises in pairs within the planes to become familiar with them. Note that there are three pairs of Openings and Closings.

8. Now practice them as pairs, using the labels of Opening and Closing, saying the words as you move.

9. When you are comfortable with the Openings and Closings, add the Shape Flow Quality labels.

10. Practice these with someone else. Performing these Openings and Closings with another person brings perspective as an observer.

11. Alternately, practice moving in opposites: for example, one Rises while the other Sinks. The dialogue with the body that is created can increase how far you can stretch to Rising or shrink to Enclosing. The action of these movements should be described with the "ing" suffix as it is a movement toward a place in Space.

12. For further exploration of these movements, imagine that you have a glass beaker that sits between your belly button and sternum. Experiment with all three pairings of Openings and Closings within the space of the beaker on your body.

13. Use the image of the beaker to represent the voluminous nature of your body. Attempting these very small changes in the mid-torso region can amplify changes that you want to happen with your ensemble.

APPLYING SHAPE FLOW QUALITIES TO THE REHEARSAL

Advancing or Retreating with the body and adding Shape Flow can change your ability to communicate with an ensemble. When you need a moment to replay a choral sound for comment, a brief moment of retreating within the body informs the ensemble that you are thinking. Whether we are engaging a person or a group as an observer/listener/teacher, we are basing all of these skills on conducting basics. We can observe ensemble intent and posture.

The listening portion is often the most crucial in relationship to intent. Conductors are, after all, teachers who must display a healthy combination of willingness to change as situations arise, with feedback both physical and intellectual. As a conductor, what are you most likely to do as you are challenged to make changes with your ensemble? Do you respond verbally or physically? Are they both important in combination? How does Spreading affect the sound when you want to change the color of your choir? Can you add richness, brightness to the sound? Does a small change in this away from your signature Shape Flow affect the ensemble?

We will, as conductors, move more readily in the upper half of the Kinesphere (Ⓚ). Does adding a sense of Rising to the mid-torso create change? Does opening the leg stance to more of a Wall allow you to support a greater sense of Advancing?

The ability to Shape can be applied in a small manner to the inner workings of the torso. The small movements practiced previously (by imagining a glass beaker within the space between the navel and the sternum) have the capacity to change your overall form. In lieu of changing the concept of posture as something that is balanced only from the back of the body and the spine, making small, mid-torso Shaping Quality changes can affect the sound of your ensemble. A small amount of rising in this area changes the perception of the ensemble that you are rising to meet their efforts. This also allows for a psychological opening toward the choir which exposes a vulnerability to allow it to give more focus and attention to the conductor. This can be important when a group is consistently reviewing and learning a passage. The wider concept of Opening and Closing applies here on a grand scale.

CONCLUSION

Your body and your intent are represented in your Shaping as an inroad to your expressivity. Shaping brings the inner intent out whether we choose to control it or not. When considering the evaluation of conductors, or even people in conversation, we are making a judgment on what we see.

How are you best using your interpretive skills? Are you someone who simply sees people as Open and Closed? Can you relate and respond effectively as a student when a teacher is Closed? Is it simply a matter of how you interpret what you see? Are there times in rehearsal when you need to find a moment of Retreating to plan your next move? Consider these questions as you experience and learn to observe more about Shape.

Chapter 5
Space

The study of movement deals with the spatial order of the paths which the limbs make in the Kinesphere, and also with the connection between outer movement and the mover's inner attitude. This attitude is not only shown in the choice of a certain path or the employment of a certain limb, but is also characterised (sic) by the choice of dynamic stresses.[31]

SPACE

The relationship between the body and the environment involves a series of common, interwoven, habitual patterns. The body creates a movement signature in how we interact with others and within the space we inhabit. How we use space gives others an interpretation of how confident we are in our surroundings from a physical and psychological perspective. It is also an indication of our own ability to move forward in controlling a situation or allowing others to take a stand.

"Space description addresses the directionality, orientation, pathways, traceforms, and spatial forms that are made visible by the body shapes and body movements."[32]

GATHERING AND SCATTERING

Theoretically, the overall concept within the area of Space and Spatial intent is Gathering and Scattering. In any given moment, we are either pulling things to us (Gathering) or Scattering, in which we give back to the environment or those around us. Our kinetic energy is shared with the space around us; we are not independent of it.

This presents a way of thinking about the role we play as conductors. The following exercise gives a series of opposites that relate to everyday life situations. Take time to experience and note how each affects you, depending on which side you are experiencing. Insert a description of your reaction to each pair of opposites below. See what images and situations come alive for you. Select one line in each pairing below and experience what you sense from these experiences. The next time you are given a compliment, consider whether you take the time to receive a sensation from it or if you are ready to give back to your environment immediately.

For example: *While Gathering compliments, I receive assurance from my environment.*

Exercises
A-1 Gathering
While Gathering compliments, I receive _____ from my environment.

—or—

While Gathering compliments, I give _____ to my environment.

A-2 Scattering
While Scattering compliments, I receive _____ from my environment.

—or—

While Scattering compliments, I give _____ to my environment.

B-1 Holding

While holding my ground in a difficult situation, I give _____ to my environment.

—or—

While holding my ground in a difficult situation, I receive _____ from my environment.

B-2 Releasing

While releasing my ground in a difficult situation I give _____ to my environment.

—or—

While releasing my ground in a difficult situation I receive _____ from my environment.

C-1 Clutching

While clutching to a creative idea and claiming it as my own I receive _____ from my environment.

—or—

While clutching to a creative idea and claiming it as my own I give _____ to my environment.

C-2 Throwing

While throwing a creative idea to others I give _____ to my environment.

—or—

While throwing a creative idea to others I receive _____ from my environment.

Write the descriptor you have filled in from each pairing above in table 5.1 below to see if you are someone who is more prone to Gathering or Scattering behavior.

EXERCISE	EXPERIENCE	RESULT	EXPERIENCE	RESULT
A	Gathering		Scattering	
B	Holding		Releasing	
C	Clutching		Throwing	

TABLE 5.1 GATHERING AND SCATTERING RESULTS

Note that as you complete this series of exercises that you might have a natural affinity to feel more comfortable on one side of the opposites practiced. This is common and simply worthy of note for your own dynamics as a conductor and teacher.

RELATIONSHIP TO CONDUCTING

Take time to experience these opposites in relationship to conducting and teaching. How might it serve you to be willing to Gather input from your ensemble prior to Scattering new directives or musical input?

Gathering and Scattering relate to the physical and psychological tasks involved in the choral rehearsal. When you want to control a tempo, a smaller gesture, tighter to the body, is typically used. This would be Gathering, or collecting the attention by bringing the gesture close to the body. Scattering, as it relates to conducting, reverses the gesture of the conductor to create a new idea and makes a change in the status of what is being rehearsed and performed. Scattering would involve indicating a cue to a section for a breath or entrance.

The use of the body to initialize spatial intent can be a powerful way to approach the rehearsal setting. A conductor must develop control over the rehearsal, and utilizing the Space aspects of LMA can give added confidence. A broader palette is created from which to work on a physical and psychological level.

CHAPTER 5 • SPACE

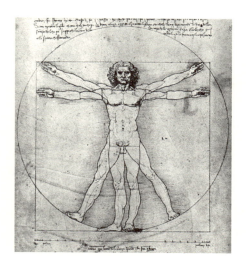

FIGURE 5.1

KINESPHERE Ⓚ

The space around us creates a personal Kinesphere that identifies how we are investing our energy in the environment. Our Kinesphere is defined by how we are experiencing movement within the space surrounding our body. Laban coined the term Kinesphere from the Greek root of "kinesis," or movement and "sphaira," which means ball.[33]

The space around the body is three-dimensional. We define our Kinesphere as the space around us that we can reach with all of our limbs while our body is in any set position. When we move the body the Kinesphere moves with us. Due to the global rotation[34] of the hip joints and arms, we are able to reach for items within a set space when grounded to the earth. Awareness of how to use and explore the Kinesphere can activate rehearsal space.

65

Observation Exercise

1. Picture a conductor with a shy demeanor on the podium. What do you envision? A closed-off body, eyes dropped and posture suggesting a lack of confidence? Do you notice the body? Perhaps what you picture is the use of the voice, less commanding, quiet and reserved?

2. Now consider the use of the space the conductor is using. Is this person aware of the spread of the limbs available? Does this person take a firm stance on the earth with both feet facing the ensemble? Does the individual stand tall from the grounded feet through the head connection?

This observation will bring answers as to the amount of Kinesphere a conductor is utilizing.

PSYCHOLOGICAL KINESPHERE

The use of space is physical and psychological. The amount of space the body is willing to take in for any given movement creates a Psychological Kinesphere. Taking control of a rehearsal situation requires confidence on a physical and psychological level. Confidence is observed and intuited by ensemble members when a conductor is prepared for rehearsal. This process includes preparation at the musical level of knowing the score, the ability to represent it with the body, and being present in the moment.

The conducting art form is the culmination of preparation and intent with the mind connected to the body. My students often say they know what they want to hear from an ensemble, but do not have the tools to make it come from the choir. Practicing awareness of the room as a whole can bring assuredness to the conductor and motivation to the singers. This practice includes opening the body to the experience.

Experience comes in listening and responding to the sound as it comes from the ensemble. Verbal and physical cues, in response to the sound produced, will create an environment that fosters trust for a healthier, more vibrant sound. There is an inherent trust an ensemble shares with a conductor that is not afraid to occupy space in the rehearsal room. Commanding space is not developed by a large body type. Small conductors can create impressive music simply by their presence. It is their capacity to foster a sense of *openness* to the situation that renders the most development in the music-making process. It is also the capacity to present the body in a large Psychological Kinesphere ((🛉)); to let it be known that the conductor has control of the situation and is not fearful of being seen as a physical representation of the musical score.

The Kinesphere is defined from a point of stability, whether from a standing, seated, or floor-based position. Spatial tensions come into play here; and they are inferred in the phrase *Approaches to Kinesphere*. Writers of LMA Theory use the phrase *Approach to Kinesphere* and *Spatial Tensions* interchangeably. This is important to note; Spatial Tensions are inferred within the movement construct, as they are the invisible pulls that occur as the body moves in one direction toward another. Table 5.2 gives three approaches as defined by Ed Groff.[35]

Approach to Kinesphere/Spatial Tension	Definition	Symbol
Central	The organization of energy that reveals the Kinesphere by radiating out and back to the center of the Kinesphere.	
Peripheral	The organization of energy that reveals the Kinesphere by identifying the edge of the Kinesphere and maintaining a sense of distance from the center of the body.	
Transverse	The organization of energy that reveals the Kinesphere by cutting through or sweeping around the space between the center and the defined edge with the center accommodating.	

TABLE 5.2 APPROACHES TO KINESPHERE

APPROACHES TO KINESPHERE

The Space of the Kinesphere is voluminous and surrounds the body like a bubble. How we move within the Kinesphere defines our Shaping (Chapter 5) and the Effort Life (Chapter 3) that gives a complete description and definition to individual movement signatures. Let us experience all three Approaches to Kinesphere.

A *Central Approach to Kinesphere* (⊘) is represented when you want to defend an opinion or idea; it is a personal movement related to your identity. The movements the body makes in this situation are small and close to the body core. You might make a small gesture with a hand, or a nod of the head to agree or disagree when you are challenged. Central Approach to Kinesphere is all about *you* and what you desire. It can be used in the rehearsal situation to control the personal dynamics of the room by bringing attention to the conductor by being small.

Peripheral Approach to Kinesphere (⊙) sets a boundary. The edge of the Kinesphere is identified through outward movements that give a concrete definition to the greatest distance the limbs can still reach and create change. As a society we practice Peripheral Approach to Kinesphere when we claim more personal space on a train or in line at the supermarket. Often a Peripheral Approach to Kinesphere can be fortified with an object that is just within arm's reach: placing a briefcase on the seat next to you on a train, or placing your shopping cart between you and another grocery customer. There are members of society that keep their Psychological Kinesphere at the Peripheral level to keep people at a professional level, not allowing individuals into their personal space. Although this is a combination of the Psychological and Physical Kinesphere, it sets the periphery just the same. The boundary is also established when young children push others on the playground to give a sense of strength; it is more about the space having strength than the individual.

A *Transverse Approach to Kinesphere* (𝒇) is a strong element in a conductor's movement signature. The conducting gesture can identify the dynamic breath of a piece and how extreme a piece can get dynamically, *piano* (*p*) or *forte* (*f*). The movements in the Transverse Approach to Kinesphere pass between the center and the edge of the Kinesphere, not addressing the edge, but moving within it. A conductor can relate the physical gesture to a Transverse movement, as there are acceptable levels of how far the gesture can reside from the body core.

When considering these situations, ask:
  1. How does Space serve you in each of these movements?
  2. How is Space a partner to your movements?

PLANES OF THE BODY

When considering the body, we can divide it into halves several ways: upper and lower, side to side, front to back. The hip joint divides the body in half from the top to the bottom. A common misconception strengthened by clothing manufacturers is that the body is split in half at the waist. Our body hinges on the rotary function of the hip joints. The halves of the body split two ways—hip joint area and down is lower; above hip joint area is upper. These two halves of the body support differing functions. The lower part supports the weight of the body and the movement of how that weight is stabilized. The upper part of the body is what we use to move. We reach and pull things to us, explore the area around us.

We also have the ability to push items away from us from that same point of stability. Moving in space requires a ride along spatial pulls. The body moves in specific directions with separate parts and limbs. When you reach for a pencil on a desk, you use your arm and hand, not your toes or head. The body is constructed to rely on spatial pulls in relation to gravity so it is not injured while completing simple tasks.

Laban identified five zones of the body: the head, two arm limbs, two leg limbs, the upper torso (which includes the head and neck), and the lower torso (which includes the lumbar segment of the spine and the pelvis). This idea was further developed in Chapter 2 by adding the tail (coccyx) to the definition of the complete body.

The three Planes of the Body are Vertical, Sagittal, and Horizontal. Laban created his movement Scales in relationship to the two-dimensional planes of the body and the three-dimensionality of the body within the Kinesphere.

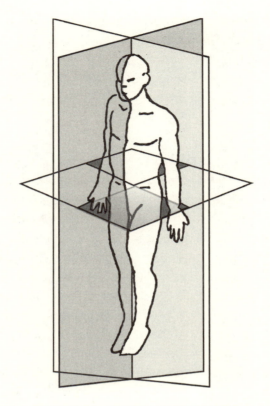

FIGURE 5.2   PLANES OF THE BODY

EXERCISES IN SPACE EXPLORATION WITH GLOBAL ROTATION, PLANES, AND BREATH

CYCLING THE PLANES

Each of the three planes has a distinct edge defined by height, breadth, and depth. Each plane has two unequal spatial pulls. These spatial pulls are supported by the two-dimensional aspect of the physical plane itself. The Vertical Plane has more height than breadth, the Horizontal has more breadth than depth, and the Sagittal Plane has more depth than height. These are defined by the natural reach space of the body. Each of these planes is experienced in a flat, two-dimensional space.

Exercise in Global Joint Rotation

This exercise will aid you in practicing shoulder girdle rotary function. This is a skill to master prior to learning Laban Scales.

1. Begin with your arm at your side. Draw the right arm into the heart center of the body, folding it in with the right hand resting at the base of the heart center (over the sternum). Your hand should curve naturally or close in a fist.

2. As you prepare to draw the arm away from the center of the sternum, notice a natural rotation that happens in the right arm.

3. Begin to drop the arm away from the body by using the first two fingers of the right hand to open the fist and rotate the arm away from the body. Initiating the movement from the fingers reinforces the need for the distal edge awareness that was practiced in Chapter 2.

4. Repeat with the left arm.

Exercise: Cycling the Planes

1. Stand positioned with the feet hip-distance apart and arms relaxed at both sides. You will cycle the planes in the order of Vertical, Sagittal, and Horizontal.

2. Begin all three cycles with the body in a neutral spine position, standing with the feet hip-distance apart under the sitz bones with the shoulders relaxed. All arm movements are initiated by an exhale for maximum range of motion. Initiate the arm movements from the scapula, keeping in mind that all healthy arm movements are initiated from this point of the body.

Vertical Plane

1. Using the right arm led by the right hand (accessing your global rotation), draw a circle in the air as large as you can while standing in place. The hand is positioned flat as if the body is a mirror which you can polish with the palm.

2. Repeat this pattern with the left arm led by the left hand, using the scapula.

Horizontal Plane

1. Using the right arm led by the right hand (accessing your global rotation), draw half an imaginary hula hoop around your core breathing mechanism (the diaphragm area) with the arm extended.

2. As you reach the back of the body, complete the drawing by leading with the left arm and hand.

3. Remember to keep the Horizontal Plane at the diaphragm level.

Sagittal Plane

1. Using the right arm led by the right hand (accessing your global rotation), draw a circle in the air as high over your head as you can reach while standing in place. The hand is positioned over the head to create a circle that begins at the top of the head and makes a ring to the floor and is completed behind you.

2. You may wish to imagine the Sagittal plane (also known as the wheel plane, because our arms move that way) as something that moves forward and back, although you should make every attempt to draw the wheel around the center of your body.

3. Repeat this pattern with the left arm led by the left hand, using the scapula.

Exercise for Connecting Breath to Movement
1. Stand positioned with the feet hip-distance apart and arms relaxed at both sides.

2. Inhale while bringing the arms in toward the breathing mechanism in a circular fashion using a Transverse Approach to Kinesphere, with the palms of the hand facing the body.

3. Imagine you are a fountain which has a water source at the abdomen.

4. As you inhale and then use your air, create larger circles into and away from the body. This scattering of your breath energy will initialize the sound of the choir you are conducting.

5. This is a reminder that an ensemble is constantly looking for representation of breath as they sing.

6. Explore this breathing technique on the floor and standing. Sensing expansion in the back of the torso while lying on the floor can bring added awareness to the depth of breath the body creates for healthy living.

SCALES

The term *scale* is used for the functional basis of proportions in art, music, and architecture. When we consider the word *scale,* there is a proportionate relationship that has been developed in relationship to the whole. Harmony creates a balance through scale design.

Musicians have an understanding of how scales within a key signature can create harmonic function to place accompaniment (harmony) underneath a melodic line. A printed musical score is divided into measures which track rhythmic structure of the overall piece. The melodic line defines the movement of the harmonic structure throughout the measure. Understanding the proportions of the melodic line allows the fingers to create a movement pattern that grants an ease of reading a piece in a specified key.

The scale has traditional proportions of whole and half steps that create a series (or pattern) that is functional and harmonic. In relationship to this, Laban has created a series of scales that can be performed with the body within the Platonic Solids to create dynamic movement that is harmonic *within* the solid and harmonic *in relationship* to how the human body is constructed.

These scales serve as a model for specific ways of moving in and through the Kinesphere. Each scale provides unique opportunities for organizing body level support, Effort phrasing, and our Shaping to fulfill spatial clarity. This text will focus on Diametral and Diagonal Scales in application to Shape and Effort for conductors.

There are lines represented by the body that *pass through* the center of the body in order for them to exist. These are called central pathways, and they define the infrastructure of the three major crystalline forms. As you learn the Defense and Diagonal Scales, you will see that your hand passes over the center of the body as it completes the movement for both of these scales. The Defense Scale follows the Body Standard Cross of Axis.

DIMENSIONAL SCALE

The Dimensional Scale is related to the area of martial arts. This scale moves around the axes of the three planes: Vertical, Sagittal, and Horizontal. This scale returns to the center of the body before it begins movement in another plane. This scale is one-dimensional and is articulated by exploring the far reach space of each plane with the upper torso in an upright position.

Laban created his sequence in following with the traditions of various cultures in martial arts he observed as a child. The Dimensional Scale was developed to create an ease of movement with efficiency. The positions traveled in the Dimensional Scale render a way to protect the most vulnerable parts of the body.

An adaptation of the Dimensional Scale is the Defense Scale, which is performed with rounded, curvilinear motions rather than the lines that are implemented in the traditional Dimensional Scale.

CHAPTER 5 • SPACE

Dimensional Scale Exercise

1. Begin with a neutral spine position, your legs shoulder distance apart, your arms relaxed at your sides. You will first experience this by the arm leading on your dominant side.

2. Imagine that there are three lines crossing through your body.

   a. One line reaches through the center of your body from top to bottom. This is your vertical axis.

   b. There is also a line that reaches from side to side; imagine that this stretches from one hip socket through to the other. This is your horizontal axis. It is important to identify the horizontal axis as pivoting through the hip joint area, as there is rotation available to you from the hip socket joints.

   c. The sagittal access runs as a line through the center of your body from front to back, and conversely back to front.

3. Before attempting this exercise, take time to identify and label the vertical, horizontal, and sagittal axes. These three axes are labeled on the Dimensional Cross of Axes.

4. With the body in a balanced position, heels under the sitz bones, raise the right arm overhead, rising to the highest point in the Kinesphere that you can reach with your feet still on the floor.

5. From this point, trace the underlying to the lowest point of the floor, moving from top to bottom. To achieve this you will need to crouch and close the body toward the floor.

6. Trace the lower half of the body and return to standing.

7. Now reach left across the body in a horizontal fashion. This will require you to enclose the body somewhat. This is considered another reach to the leftmost part of the Kinesphere that you can reach while still keeping your feet grounded on the floor.

8. To return in the opposite fashion as to pull, trace with your right hand across the center of the body and return your arm to the right side into the Kinesphere in the Horizontal plane.

9. Return the right hand to the center of the body at the back side of the torso, and reach back to the space behind you in the Sagittal plane.

10. As you cannot put your hand through the center of the body physically, as you bring the right hand back in toward the body, bring it around the right side of the torso to pull the body toward the front of the Sagittal plane.

11. To complete the scale, return the hand to the center of the body and then relax at the right side.

12. This scale will later relate to Rising, Sinking, Enclosing, Spreading, Retreating, and Advancing. These terms can help you in activating the Defense Scale.

13. Consider speaking the word *Rising* as you move upward, *Sinking* as you drop toward the floor in an upright position.

14. Continue by Enclosing the body in order to cross the body center, this time using your hand and closing in the right foot. The opposite of this is to spread the arm and body open in the Horizontal plane.

15. The last two shaping styles you will use to complete the Defense Scale are to Retreat and Advance.

16. Retreating is achieved by allowing the body to curve at the spinal level toward the back of the body while the hand rests at the abdomen.

17. Advancing is achieved by pulling an imaginary string from the torso to bring the body back to balance in the arm to the far reach space in the Sagittal Plane.

SYMBOLS FOR THE BODY IN SPACE

Laban designed symbols to indicate specific places to mark the body in space. The center of your body is place middle ( ). The top of the body over the head is place high ( ), while the space your feet occupy at ground level is place low ( ). *To mark the edges of the cube in far reach space, reach as far as you can with your distal edges.* The labels of the body are given in the combination order of where you are headed (right or left), the direction (forward, back, side) and the place level (high, middle, or low).

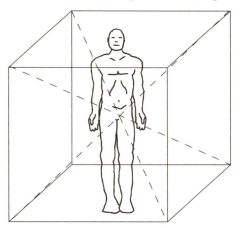

FIGURE 5.3 MOVEMENT IN THE CUBE

EXPLORATION OF MOVEMENT IN THE CUBE

The Movement in the Cube will be led with the right hand leading the following exercise. To reach to the top right front of the cube with your right hand, you would say you are reaching right, forward, high. To make a diagonal line from this corner to the lower *opposite* corner behind you would be to move across the body to arrive at left, back, low. This diagonal can also be traveled in the opposite direction from left, back, low to right, forward, high.

The other pathway to trace within the cube is from left, forward, high to right, back, low. By traveling the opposite of this new pathway from right, back, low to left, forward, high completes the lines of the cube. You will now explore the full Diagonal Scale within the Cube.

Picture yourself with imaginary lines that cross through the body from the opposite corner of the cube to the other. For example, the forward upper right corner reaches to the back, lower, left corner and passes through the body. The opposite—the forward, upper, left corner reaches to the back, right corner. This makes a large X inside the cube. The Diagonal Scale gives you a way to travel these from each corner of the cube in succession.

Diagonal Scale

Imagine that your body is standing in the middle of the cube; reaching to the right is one flat, square edge, to the left another. The square encompasses the whole of the body, not simply the reach space of the hand. The body is standing on the base of the cube, while there is also a flat edge above the head. The third side of the cube is flat behind you and flat in front of you. These three sides relate to the three planes we have previously explored.

You will move *within* the cube to explore the diagonal reach that happens from one corner of the cube to the other, hence it is called the Diagonal Scale. Exploring this scale will model the capacity you have for extreme movement from a central point of rest. This relates to conducting as we use our breathing core to sustain and support all of our potential movement in rehearsal. Understanding the relationship between the body and the use of space in the rehearsal setting will build strength and response from your ensemble.

You will use the right hand to trace the scale to learn the pattern, but may later reverse the scale to use the left hand as the leading arm to trace the form.

You will begin by reaching the right hand to the right, forward, high position and then trace the invisible line of the X to the lower opposite corner at left, back, low. Your body will naturally enclose into the arm as

CHAPTER 5 • SPACE

you move lower in your Kinesphere ((K)), and rise when you move higher from a lower position.

Next, bring the arm to the left, forward, high position and trace the invisible line to the lower opposite corner at right, back, low. *Reminder: the body stays facing forward for this scale as much as possible. (This will help to relate this to conducting when we combine Full Effort Actions with this Scale in chapter 6.)*

Raise the arm to right, back, high to prepare for the new movement. The second half of the scale begins at the back, right corner of the cube, which is labeled right, back, high. You will continue to trace the line of the X to the opposite corner, left, front, low. Return the hand to the center position and take the right hand to left, back, high. You will now complete the scale by tracing the imaginary X line from left, back, high to right, forward, low. At the completion of the scale you will bring the arm back to place middle (·).

Chapter 6
Thematic Application

THEMATIC APPLICATION
OF LABAN MOVEMENT ANALYSIS

The Concepts of Inner-Outer, Stability-Mobility, and Function-Expression are foundational concepts of the twelve Principles of the Bartenieff Fundamentals found in Peggy Hackney's text, *Making Connections: Total Body Integration Through Bartenieff Fundamentals*. These ideas are primary ways to explore your own way to practice, indwell, and find meaning for your life in general and in movement work. Integrated Movement Studies (IMS) uses these fundamental truths as a structure for their certification program classes.

Our movement signature is an undeniable indicator of how we think on the inside and how we relate outwardly toward situations and the people that surround us.

Conductors can use Bartenieff and other IMS principles to plan rehearsals, but also to live a full life as a professional educator. Taking the time to experience these principles will bring change to your life, both personally and professionally, showing ways to live a well-balanced life in relating to others and finding calm within yourself.

Success in applying any of the concepts of this text to your rehearsal style, movement signature, and body health comes from exploring these exercises frequently. CLMA practitioners use Bartenieff Fundamentals sequences to prepare for daily life and teaching. Developed over time, the ideas of the Laban system will enliven the body in preparation for the next day or task. Use this chapter to reflect and explore how these concepts can assist you in your journey to becoming a more proficient and expressive conductor.

INNER-OUTER

The principle of Inner-Outer relates to how we use our inner impulses to affect the outer world around us. Receiving information from our actions, in turn, affects how we think on the inside. Such Inner-Outer relationships are a fundamental of the Laban system. All the movements we make as conductors affect the lives and responses of the performers in our ensembles. We create personal meaning with the postures and gestures we use on a daily basis.

The use of imagery with choral warm-ups can enliven the ensemble, whether it is a story or a physical gesture. Consider your Effort Life as you prepare for rehearsals. Using inner emotions to help with an expressive line in a score can bring shape to the phrase. Having intent for what you want to hear, a sense of expectation, will give the choir something to aspire to achieve.

Eph Ehly, one of my choral conducting mentors, is the most brilliant motivator of this technique I have seen. He can tell a story with an Effortful voice and body which changes the mood of the rehearsal room. It is through his mental vision and how he moves the singers through his vision that he achieves such miraculous results. This is an achievable result for all conductors if preparation and imagery are used in the score study process. Applying areas of relationship to how a line *feels* when sung, as well as how it *sounds*, can give students a new perspective on how to perform a piece.

Journal Exercise in Inner-Outer

Ask yourself the following questions regarding the rehearsal situation, both as an ensemble member and conductor.

1. What are your inner impulses in performing?

2. How does taking in the environment and revealing what you see around you in rehearsal help you to be a more consummate musician?

3. What do you notice about your Body Connectivity when you first start rehearsal?

4. Are you considering the Effort Life you are using in your tone of voice as you sing or give directions?

5. Do you use imagery for yourself when thinking about the color of sound that you want from your voice/ensemble?

6. What images are you using to develop a warm-up for your singing/conducting, using a combination of Body and Shape concepts?

Save your answers for these questions for future reinvestment. Over time, you may find that situations and circumstances change your answers.

STABILITY-MOBILITY

The concept of Stability-Mobility explains a natural phrasing in movement, activated by kinetic chains and moving from moments of Stability to moments of Mobility. Stability supports moments of grounding that then allow the body to experience heightened movements of Mobility. *Stability is* not *about bracing or holding the body tense*, but about allowing energy to travel through the core to the outer parts of the body for expression. Stability is encouraged by intent to move to a vast array of choices because *grounding gives support*. Mobility, on the other hand, is supported by the

Stability that precedes it, although Mobility is often the motivator to find a sense of Stability in the body.

The ability to dance and move your body during score study will often bring heightened awareness of how stable you must be in your core in order for Mobility to have a rooted foundation. This foundation can support a great array of movement possibilities if the foundation is rooted in breath and support of the entire torso.

Knowing your intention can inform the Effortful way you approach the environment. As a conductor, you must be aware of the body balance and use of Space on the podium. When rehearsing with a group for the first time, take time in the warm-up sequence to test the boundaries of how Effortful you can be and still have a positive response. In the early weeks of rehearsal, a good foundation of Stability-Mobility will encourage the singers to participate fully and with good intent.

SHAPE

Stability-Mobility has numerous applications to Shape. In fact, moving within the Modes of Shape Change requires a base understanding of Stability-Mobility.

Why is there sometimes no sense of the individual in movement? Beginning conducting students initially use Directional Movement (—↛) as the primary way to inspire Mobility in a choir. Directionality is imperative, but beginning students often lack a Shape Flow Support (—↛) moment to check their body for the inner intent inspiration. Such a moment of Stability gives the conductor focus to achieve the most artistic results possible, because the body is supported.

Even many experienced conductors choose to mimic the gestural style of a colleague or mentor rather than develop their own style. It is my hope that, through the training in this text, you will develop a unique style that is body specific and enhances your own movement signature.

As a conductor, the ability to analyze and change your Shape gives you great flexibility in how to approach the rehearsal. Investing in the decision-making process during rehearsal through Stability in Shape Flow Support (—↛) can create beautiful phrases of Mobility by engaging in

Carving (~o). The co-creative process that gives a conductor insight into his community and its responses to his gestures can alter his life on the podium. Conducting is *in reaction and relationship to* the choir that is singing. Without an inner sense of who she is and what she wants, supported by Shape Flow Support (—*—), the conductor will not have the ability to Mobilize in a co-creative way and respond to the creative beings in the ensemble.

STABILITY-MOBILITY USING BODY/BARTENIEFF FUNDAMENTALS

The application of Stability-Mobility to the Bartenieff Fundamentals supports all six Patterns of Total Body Connectivity: Breath, Core-Distal, Upper-Lower, Head-Tail, Body Half, and Cross-Lateral. There are moments in all patterns where Mobility is actualized to encourage meaningful movement. This Mobility is supported by Stability that is grounded in a relationship to the earth. Reaching out from that source of strength and support to the environment, conductors can live creative and individual lives that are dynamically unique.

Though the principle of Stability-Mobility can be applied to each of the Connectivity Patterns, the overarching concept of Yield & Push from the Head-Tail Connectivity Pattern (⑧) is the primary application. In addition, Reach & Pull gives the body the opportunity to reach into space and out into the world, which can be a metaphor for Mobility, since Mobility has options for many creative movements. Below is one example of Stability-Mobility as a principle in all Six Patterns of Total Body Connectivity.

Breath Connectivity (⑧) Exercise
1. Imagine that all of your cells are dripping into the floor as you observe the physical sensation of just being in the moment as a breathing creature. You are supported by the Stability of the earth and your relationship to it with your own boney landmarks and sinewy, gooey tissue.

2. As you feel the urge to ooze into the floor and move to a new position to find a renewed sense of comfort (as babies do in the womb), you are briefly Mobile.

3. This concept can be applied to daily meditation practice, realizing that the Breath (⑧) is supported by the earth and the body.

CORE-DISTAL CONNECTIVITY (⋈)

Core-Distal Connectivity (⋈) is experienced as a Pattern by recognizing that all six limbs of the torso have a relationship to and through the core of the body. Stability is recognized in this Pattern as the core. There is support of any creative movement in Mobility by tracing the connection of one of the six limbs to the core.

HEAD-TAIL CONNECTIVITY (⑧)

Head-Tail Connectivity (⑧) is related, as stated earlier, to the concept of Yield & Push. This is the idea that we Yield into the earth to find gravity (Stability) for support, and can then Push out from that strength to move into the world (Mobility). The Yield gives an individual identity that has movement potential actualized through a Push from the lower body through to an upper distal limb. The following basic exercise from Peggy Hackney's book, *Making Connections,* helps explain the Head-Tail (⑧) Connection.

Head-Tail Connection Exercise
1. Come up onto the knees and forearms for support (Stability) to roll the head on the earth and roll the tail in the air as well.

2. This through-line is often identified as the Pattern that is most likely to inhibit true expressivity for movement artists at all levels.

3. Often the tail is not trained to have a connection as a separate limb to the core.

4. An evocative image that can be used to find the Head-Tail Connection (⊗) is the spine being made of a very gooey chain that has a tail which moves the head.

5. The feet-to-head and arms-to-tail connections intensify and engage this Pattern.

UPPER-LOWER CONNECTIVITY (⊗)

Upper-Lower Connectivity (-⊗-) is another way to practice Stability-Mobility. Yield & Push (the sense of self identified above under Head-Tail (⊗) Connectivity) can be considered the Stability. In relationship, the Reach and Pull Pattern that naturally follows this progression of movement is a reach into the environment to bring something to you; this creates moments of Mobility. Rotary function for Mobility, from a relaxed scapula in Stability, can give student conductors a way to explore a more creative and easeful connection for Carving (~∞).

BODY-HALF CONNECTIVITY (⊕)

Body-Half Connectivity (⊕) utilizes moments of Stability on one side of the body to promote Mobility and movement on the other. This is *key* for working with beginning conductors, because they learn to keep traditional conducting patterns with the right side of the body and identify the dynamic shaping of the musical phrase with the left. Depending on the sidedness of the student, either the pattern or expressive hand can be Stability or Mobility. Experiment with your body as you decide which side is dominant and can support the other for creative Mobility.

CROSS-LATERAL CONNECTIVITY (⊗)

Cross-Lateral Connectivity (⊗) can manifest the most creative situation in the body for Mobility. This pattern supports Mobilization by walking and cross-body crawling in infants.

Consider the body as a large X; one side of the X becomes the Stability, the other Mobility. This diagonal dynamism can be experienced by conductors with the arm circle. To engage the support of opposing limbs such as the right arm to left leg (Mobility), Stability must be engaged in the opposing limbs through core. As this is the most developed pattern, it supports the most Mobility from the core to the limbs. Practice all of these patterns from time to time in order to engage your choirs in a healthy and expressive experience.

Exercise for Stability-Mobility using Space Harmony

Stability-Mobility in relationship to Space Harmony can be practiced through any of the scales. To practice the Diagonal Scale given in Chapter 5, review the material on scale and reinvest your body energy in moving. Once you have reviewed the scale, continue with your reading for the following reminders as you apply the concept of Stability-Mobility.

1. In any arrival point in the Diagonal Scale, you must establish Stability in the core and through the counter-tension of the opposite arm to allow full movement and move to a point of Stability.

2. Consider that the points through which you travel do have brief movements of Stability. By moving through one reach to another, you are also promoting Mobility in your entire body, not just the arms or torso.

3. As you reach the end of each arrival point in the scale, you have a moment of Stability that will aid in the re-initiation of the next destination point and the continuity for performing the balance of the scale with the same dynamism.

4. Realize that there must be moments of connection through the body to the distal edges to maximize the movement potential of the scale.

5. You must ride the Spatial Pulls[36] and know where your body is going at all times.

6. How does Stability-Mobility improve your ability to perform the Diagonal Scale?

7. An active feet-to-head connection gives the conductor more facility to establish Stable points in the gesture when the body is connected to core.

DIAGONAL SCALE WITH EFFORT ELEMENTS IN COMBINATION

Now that you have reviewed the Diagonal Scale, you can add the Effort Elements in Combination to the movement pattern for advanced practice in combining Space and Effort. Beginning with a move toward right, forward, high, add Float ( ) at the arrival point. Continue through the Diagonal scale, adding the Effort Elements in Combination in the order of Float ( ), Punch ( ), Glide ( ), Slash ( ), Dab ( ), Wring ( ), Flick ( ), and Press ( ). Notice as you move, that these movements will also create opposites of Openings and Closings for the first two pairs (Float and Punch, Glide and Slash) and then Closings and Openings for the second pair (Dab and Wring, Flick and Press).

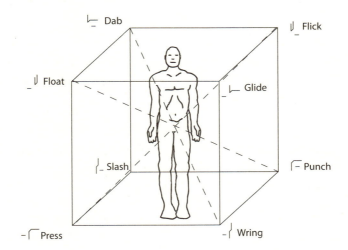

FIGURE 6.1: EFFORT ACTIONS IN THE CUBE

FUNCTION-EXPRESSION

Functional and expressive aspects of movement are in an intimate relationship.[37]

The integration between Function and Expression creates a relationship by using basic body patterns and knowledge to create an artistic moment. All movement has meaning. The artistic and expressive aspects of moving can come from sensation, developing a good sound from your choir, or simply initiating the willingness to rehearse on an expressive level. Our movements as conductors are seen both as moments of Function and Expression. Conductors practice basic patterns to inform the ensemble of tempo and meter, and then expressive aspects of a score. Consider that expressive aspects can be shown through body posture, intent, and gesture. How would that change intent toward creating and practicing gestures for a rehearsal or performance?

Journal Exercise

Using the thematic areas of the LMA system, explore all the ways you can improve the body as you prepare the score for rehearsal and performance. Consider one of these questions prior to a rehearsal or conducting class and keep a journal of your responses. Notice if any of the components of LMA consistently capture your awareness.

1. Consider all of the Patterns of Total Body Connectivity. Did you learn to identify what patterns make you most connected? Do you work for a grounded core and buoyant posture consistently?

2. Do you have self-awareness of the Shaping of your arms or the connection to the scapula to free the arm for Carving?

3. Are you aware of the expressive uses of the Psychological Kinesphere? Your sense of awareness—is this Function or Expression to you?

4. At the moment of breath initiation for the choir, are you aware of the Function you are using to prepare for the Expression to follow?

5. Are you aware of your Effort Life as you give directions?

6. Do you have Full Effort Actions that have become a part of your gestural vocabulary?

7. Do you use Shape Flow Support to alter the sound and color your ensemble is producing?

8. How can the overall ideas of this book move you from Function to Expression?

9. Do you move from Function to Expression, or cycle back to initiate a higher level of Function for you as a conductor? Function equals Expression equals Function. The idea is that Expression breeds a *higher* level of Function.

CONCLUSION

Movement is a vital aspect of how we as humans communicate. Our movement signature is unique and gives us the ability to relate with others on many levels. As individuals, we can make a conscious decision to live an Effortful, balanced, and expressive life. As conductors, we are fortunate to have ways to express ourselves from the mind through the body to the artistic moment in relationship to an ensemble.

Once a conductor is less self-aware of her patterns and more aware of the sound coming from the ensemble, gestures will become more of a response to the sound and a co-creative process in relationship. The foundation of a physically healthy and emotionally successful rehearsal is the relationship that is built between the ensemble and the conductor. Bringing self-awareness and practice to all of the possibilities that have been introduced here will give the student conductor a good foundation for conducting study.

Because the LMA system is individualized, conductors can refine their personal visions by exploring the system in tandem or in isolation. The system is also easy to review as a whole or in parts as they seem most relevant. It is my hope that you will take the time to explore all of these parts of the system over time.

Endnotes

1. Michele Menard Holt, "The Application to Conducting and Choral Rehearsal Pedagogy of Laban Effort/Shape and Its Comparative Effect upon Style in Choral Performance (Conducting Pedagogy)," *DMA dissertation* (University of Hartford, 1992), 29. Rudolf Laban, *A Life for Dance*, trans. Lisa Ullman (London: MacDonald and Evans Limited, 1975).
2. Dervish dancing is a prayer performed by Moslem lay-brothers who offer their prayers in a continuous spinning of the body.
3. Rudolf Laban, *A Life for Dance*, trans. and annotated Vera Maletic, *Body Space Expression* (New York: Mouten de Groyter, 1987). Lisa Ullman (London: MacDonald and Evans Limited, 1975).
4. Laban, *A Life for Dance*, 56.
5. Mark Thornton, *Laban International Courses*, March 2, 2001, http://freespace.virgin.net/ mark.thornton/abtlbn.htm. Taken from *A Movement Perspective of Rudolf Laban*, no longer in print.
6. Valerie Preston-Dunlop, *Rudolf Laban: An Extraordinary Life* (London: Dance Books Ltd., 1998).
7. Preston-Dunlop, 196.
8. Preston-Dunlop, 199.
9. Preston-Dunlop, 199.
10. Worker motions were also adapted for efficiency by creating movement patterns that were equally possible for men and women, who were a core of the industrial work force at the time.
11. Preston-Dunlop, 199.
12. Preston-Dunlop, 131–132.
13. Preston-Dunlop, 133.
14. Hutchinson was anxious to adapt Laban's notational system and add some of her own insights to her teaching.
15. Laban often corresponded with Hutchinson and had disagreements as well.
16. Peggy Hackney, "Making Connections through Bartenieff Fundamentals" (1995), 3. Handout.

17 Peggy Hackney, *Total Body Integration through Bartenieff Fundamentals* (New York: Routledge, 2002).
18 Moving in mirror image means that while one faces another, the opposing sides of the body move. For example, a conductor moves with the right hand while the singers move with the left.
19 Kinesphere is the boundary outside the body that is established by the far reach space of all limbs from the torso. This boundary gives a parameter for how high, forward, backward, and deep a person can reach.
20 Hackney, "Making Connections," 41.
21 Hackney, "Making Connections," 121.
22 Hackney, "Making Connections," 166.
23 Rudolf Laban, *The Mastery of Movement* (London: Macdonald & Evans, 1971), 8.
24 Ed Groff, "Laban Movement Analysis: An Historical, Philosophical and Theoretical Perspective," Masters thesis, Connecticut College (New London, CT, 1990).
25 In CLMA training, there is a great deal of work in understanding the physical boundaries and movement potential that can be explored by the series of scales that Laban created in relation to movement within the Platonic Solids.
26 A core member of the IMS faculty. His definition comes from my IMS Certification class notes.
27 Used with permission from Ed Groff.
28 It is important to note that Leslie Bishko and Pam Schick developed these symbols, according to Hackney, "Making Connections," 228.
29 Peggy Hackney, "Handout from IMS Certification Program" (2001).
30 These symbols have been developed recently and are used within the IMS Program. The Shape Action stroke is through the center of each symbol.
31 Rudolf Laban, *The Language of Movement: A Guidebook to Choreutics*, ed. and annotated by Lisa Ullmann (Boston, MA: Plays, Inc. Publishing, 1974), 27.
32 Groff, 139.
33 Vera Maletic, *Body Space Expression* (New York: Mouten de Groyter, 1987), 59.
34 The three-dimensional rotation of the shoulder girdle.

35 One of the researchers in this area.
36 We talk in Laban terms about riding Spatial Pulls—that it is more of a consistent movement or continuum.
37 Hackney, "Making Connections," 45.

Bibliography

Bainbridge-Cohen, Bonnie. *Sensing, Feeling, and Action: The Experiential Anatomy of Body-Mind Centering*. Northampton, MA: Contact Editions, 1993.

Barteneiff, Irmgard with Dori Lewis. *Body Movement: Coping with the Environment*. New York, NY: Gordon and Breach Science Publishers, 1980.

Barteneiff, Irmgard, and Martha Lewis. "The Unity of Expression and Function." *Research Approaches to Movement and Personality*. New York, NY: Arno Press, 1972.

Benge, Timothy John. "Movements Utilized by Conductors in the Stimulation of Expression and Musicianship." DMA dissertation, University of Southern California, 1996.

Billingham, Lisa Adalade. "The Development of a Gestural Vocabulary for Choral Conductors Based on the Movement Theory of Rudolf Laban." DMA dissertation, University of Arizona, 2001.

Davies, Eden. *Beyond Dance: Laban's Legacy of Movement Analysis*. London: Brechin Books, Ltd., 2001.

Dell, Cecily. *A Primer for Movement Description*. New York, NY: Dance Notation Bureau Press, 1970.

Foster, John. *The Influences of Rudolf Laban*. London: Lepus Books, 1977.

Goldman, Ellen. *As Others See Us: Body Movement and the Art of Successful Communication*. Gordon and Breach, 1994.

Groff, Ed. "Laban Movement Analysis: An Historical, Philosophical and Theoretical Perspective." Masters thesis, Connecticut College, New London, CT, 1990.

Groff, Ed. "Laban Movement Analysis: Charting the Ineffable Domain of Human Movement." *Journal of Physical Education, Recreation & Dance* (American Alliance for Health, Physical Education, Recreation and Dance) 66 (February 1995): 27–30.

Hackney, Peggy. "Handout from IMS Certification Program." 2001.

—. "Making Connections through Bartenieff Fundamentals." 1995.

—. *Making Connections: Total Body Integration through Bartenieff Fundamentals*. New York: Routledge, 1998, 2002.

—. *Total Body Integration through Bartenieff Fundamentals*. New York: Routledge, 2002.

Hibbard, Therees Tkach. "The Use of Movement as an Instructional Technique in Choral Rehearsals." DMA dissertation, University of Oregon, 1994.

Hodgson, John. *Mastering Movement: The Life and Work of Rudolf Laban*. New York, NY: Routledge, 2001.

Hodgson, John, and Valerie Preston-Dunlop. *Rudolf Laban: An Introduction to His Work and Influence*. Plymouth, MA: Northcote House Publishers, 1990.

Holt, Michele Menard. "The Application to Conducting and Choral Rehearsal Pedagogy of Laban Effort/Shape and Its Comparative Effect upon Style in Choral Performance (Conducting Pedagogy)." DMA dissertation, University of Hartford, 1992.

Hutchinson, Ann. *Labanotation*. New York, NY: Theatre Arts Books, 1954.

Jordan, James M. "The Effects of Informal Movement Instruction Derived from the Theories of Rudolf van Laban upon the Rhythm Performance and Discrimination of High School Students." PhD dissertation, Temple University, 1986.

Kestenberg, Judith S. *Role of Movement Patterns in Development*. New York, NY: Dance Notation Bureau Press, 1977.

Laban, Rudolf. *A Life for Dance*. Translated by Lisa Ullman. London: MacDonald and Evans Limited, 1975.

Laban, Rudolf, and F. C. Lawrence. *Effort: Economy of Human Movement*. 2nd edition. MacDonald and Evans Limited, 1974.

Laban, Rudolf. *Modern Educational Dance*. 3rd edition. Edited and revised by Lisa Ullman. MacDonald and Evans, 1975.

—. *The Language of Movement: A Guidebook to Choreutics*. Annotated and edited by Lisa Ullmann. Boston, MA: Plays, Inc. Publishing, 1974.

—. *The Mastery of Movement*. London: MacDonald & Evans, 1971.

—. *The Mastery of Movement*. 3rd edition. Boston: Plays, Inc. Publishing, 1971.

Lewis, Barbara. "Movement and Music Education: An Historian's Perspective." *Philosophy of Music Education Review*, Fall 1998: 113–123.

Loman, Susan, and Rose Brandt. *The Body-Mind Connection in Human Movement Analysis*. Keene, NH: Antioch New England Graduate School, 1992.

Lonis, Dale. "Development and Application of a Model for the Teaching of Conducting Gestures." EdD dissertation, University of Illinois at Champaign-Urbana, 1993.

Maletic, Vera. *Body Space Expression*. New York: Mouten de Groyter, 1987.

McCaw, Dick. *An Eye for Movement: Warren Lamb's Career in Movement Analysis*. London: Brechin Books Limited, 2006.

Miller, Stephen W. A. "The Effect of Laban Movement on the Ability of Student Conductors to Communicate through Gesture." PhD dissertation, University of Wisconsin-Madison, 1988.

Moore, Carol-Lynne. *Movement and Making Decisions: The Body-Mind Connection in the Workplace*. New York, NY: Rosen Book Works, Inc., 2005.

Moore, Carol-Lynne, and Kaoru Yamamoto. *Beyond Words: Movement Observation and Analysis*. New York, NY: Routledge, 1988.

Partsch-Bergsohn, Isa. *Modern Dance in Germany and the United States: Crosscurrents and Influences*. VHS. Produced by Routledge, 1994.

Preston-Dunlop, Valerie. *Rudolf Laban: An Extraordinary Life*. London: Dance Books Ltd., 1998.

Sellers-Young, Barbara. *Breathing, Movement, Exploration*. New York, NY: Applause Theatre & Cinema Books, 2001.

Souriau, Paul. *The Aesthetics of Movement*. Amherst, MA: University of Massachusetts Press, 1983.

Thornton, Mark. *Laban International Courses*.

Wis, Ramona M. "Gesture and Body Movement as Physical Metaphor to Facilitate Learning and Enhance Musical Experience in the Choral Rehearsal." PhD dissertation, Northwestern University, 1993.

INDEX

A

Action Drive. 37
Advancing 56, 57, 58, 59, 76, 77
An Eye for Movement. 48
AO Joint. 18, 25
Approaches to Kinesphere 67, 68
Arcing 54
Arms-to-Tail Connection 87
Art of Movement Studio 5, 48
Ascona 3
Asymmetric Tonic Neck Reflex
(ATNR). 24

B

Bainbridge-Cohen, Bonnie 10, 11
Ball. 52
Bartenieff Fundamentals 9, 23,
81, 82, 85
Bartenieff, Irmgard. 6, 9, 10, 48, 81
Bereska, Dussia 7
Bishko, Leslie 94
Body. 83
Body Connectivity 10, 83
Body Standard Cross of Axis. 74
Body-Half 24, 25, 85
Body-Half Connectivity. . . .10, 11, 87
Body-Half Patterning. 23, 24
Bound Flow 32, 33, 35
Breath. 10, 11, 12, 30, 85, 86
breath ball. 14
Breath Connectivity 83
Breath Patterning 26, 30

C

Carving. 29, 53, 54, 55, 85, 87, 90
Central Approach
to Kinesphere 67, 68
Certified Laban Movement Analysis
(CLMA) 9, 19, 37
Closed 49, 51, 59
Closed body 49
Closing. .48, 49, 50, 51, 57, 58, 59, 89
Clutching .63
Complete Effort Actions 44, 45
Core-Distal. 85
Core-Distal Connectivity 10, 11, 15, 86
Core-Distal Patterning 16
counter-tension. 88
Cross-Lateral 28, 30, 85
Cross-Lateral Connectivity . . . 10, 11,
27, 28, 29, 87
Cross-Lateral Patterning 27, 29
Cycling the planes 70, 71
Cube. 77, 78, 89

D

Da Vinci 52
Dab. 39, 40, 44, 89
Defense Scale. 74, 76
Dervish dancing. 93
Diagonal. 74, 78, 79, 88, 89
Diametral Scales 74

Die Welt des Tänzers (The Dancer's
    World). 3
Dimensional Cross of Axes 56, 75
Dimensional Scale 74, 75, 76
Direct Space. 33, 34, 36,
        37, 41, 42, 43
Directional 53, 54
Directional Mode of Shape Change 54
Directional Movement 84
Directional Shape Change 54
Directionality 82
Distal edges 15, 16, 17, 18,
        25, 29, 30, 77
Drives. 37

E

Effort 6, 31, 45, 74, 89
Effort Action 37, 39
Effort Actions in Combination. .38, 41
Effort Actions in opposite pairs 40
Effort Elements 31, 34, 37, 38
Effort Elements in Combination . . 37,
        40, 89
Effort Life . .34, 43, 44, 68, 82, 83, 90
Effort Phrasing. 74
Ehly, Eph 82
Ein Leben für den Tanz (A Life for
    Dance). 4
Enclosing 56, 57, 76
Expression 90, 91
extension 24, 48

F

factory workers 48
Feet-to-Head Connection. 87
femoral flexion. 20, 22
flexion 24, 48
Flick 39, 40, 44, 89
Float 39, 40, 89
Flow 31, 34, 37, 44
Free Flow 32, 33, 34
Full Effort Actions 37, 44, 79, 91
Function. 90, 91
Function-Expression 81, 90

G

Gathering 62, 63, 64
Glide. 39, 40, 89
Global Joint Rotation. 71
global rotation 65, 72
Goebbels .5
Groff, Ed 6, 48, 67, 94
Grounding 22, 28, 29, 83

H

Hackney, Peggy 6, 10, 11,
        37, 53, 81, 86, 93, 94
Head-Tail 18, 85, 86
Head-Tail Connection 86, 87
Head-Tail Connectivity 10, 11,
        26, 85, 86
Head-Tail Patterning 17
Hoberman Sphere. 14
Holding .63

Horizontal 19, 26, 56,
          70, 71, 72, 74, 76
Horizontal axis................75
Horizontal plane.......56, 57, 72, 76
Hutchinson, Anne.........6, 7, 8, 91

I

Indirect Space...33, 34, 36, 41, 43, 45
inner and outer connectivity.......19
inner attitude 53, 61
inner intent.......... 10, 19, 35, 45,
                53, 54, 59, 84
Inner-Outer..............81, 82, 83
Integrated Movement Studies
    (IMS)....................6, 81
intent 58

J-K

Joos, Kurt..................4, 5, 7
Kestenberg, Judith 48
Kinesphere.......... 17, 58, 61, 65,
    66, 67, 68, 70, 74, 75, 76, 79, 94
kinetic chains...................83
Kinetographie 7, 8
Kinetographie Laban.............8
Knust, Albrecht 7, 8

L

Laban Institute of Movement Studies
    (LIMS)..................6, 9
Laban Movement Analysis
    (LMA)..........6, 9, 48, 90, 92
Laban Movement Theory.........37

Laban, Rudolph 1, 2, 5, 6, 9, 48
Labanotation 6, 7, 8
Lamb, Warren................6, 48
Lawrence, F.C................6, 48
Leeder, Sigrid...............4, 5, 7
Light Weight..........33, 35, 40, 45
Location-oriented Shape Change...54

M

*Making Connections: Total Body
    Integration through Bartenieff
    Fundamentals*............79, 84
martial arts 74
McCaw, Dick 48
Meaden, Janice..................6
meditation 12, 13, 86
Mobility 83, 84, 85, 86, 87, 88
Mobilization...................87
Modern Educational Dance........5
Modes of Shape Change 29, 53,
                    54, 84
movement choir 2, 3
Movement Pattern Analysis.......48
movement signature...... 12, 31, 32,
        34, 37, 40, 45, 61, 68,
                81, 82, 84, 91

N-O

Notation 6, 7
ontogenetic....................10
Open..................49, 51, 59
Open body 49

103

Opening 48, 49, 50, 51,
57, 58, 59, 89

P

Patterns of Total Body Connectivity
    (PTBC) . . 10, 11, 12, 19, 29, 85, 90
Peripheral Approach
    to Kinesphere 67, 68
phyrogenetic development 10, 11
Physical Kinesphere. 68
Pin 52
planes 19, 26, 56, 57, 70
Platonic Solids 47, 48, 74, 94
posture 58, 59, 90
Press 39, 89
Principles of the Bartenieff
    Fundamentals 79
Psychological Kinesphere 37, 66,
67, 68, 90
PTBC exercises 12
Punch 39, 89

Q-R

Quick Time. 32, 33, 36, 45
Reach & Pull 85, 87
Releasing 63
Retreating. 56, 57, 58, 59, 76
Rising 55, 56, 57, 58, 76
rotary function 69, 71, 89

S

Sagittal 19, 26, 56, 70, 71, 74
Sagittal axis 75
Sagittal Plane 57, 72, 76
Scale. 47, 48, 70, 73, 74
Scattering 62, 63, 64
Schick, Pam 6, 94
Screw 52
Shape 14, 47, 48, 51,
53, 58, 59, 74, 83, 84
Shape Flow. . 14, 50, 53, 54, 56, 57, 58
Shape Flow Qualities 56, 58
Shape Flow Support. . . . 55, 84, 85, 91
Shape Forms. 52
Shaping 55, 59, 68, 74, 90
Shaping Quality 59
Sinking. 56, 57, 76
Slash. 38, 39, 89
Space 31, 34, 36, 37, 39, 41,
57, 61, 62, 64, 69, 84, 89
Space Harmony 47, 88
spatial intent. 62, 64
Spatial Pulls 70, 88, 95
Spatial tensions 67
Spoke-like Directional Mode
    of Shape Change. 54
Spoking 54, 55
Spreading 56, 57, 58, 76
Stability 70, 83, 84, 85, 86, 87, 88
Stability-Mobility. 23, 81, 83,
84, 85, 87, 88
States 37
Static forms 52
Strong Weight. 33, 35, 38, 45

Sustained Time........32, 33, 35, 36
Symbol......................39

T

Tetrahedron 47, 52
Throwing 63
Time....31, 32, 34, 35, 36, 37, 39, 41
Traverse Approach
    to Kinesphere 67, 68, 73

U

Ullman, Lisa....................5
Upper-Lower 22, 85
Upper-Lower Connectivity ... 10, 11, 26, 87
Upper-Lower Patterning..........19

V

Vertical. .19, 26, 56, 57, 70, 71, 72, 74
Vertical axis 75
Vertical plane 56, 70, 72

W

Wall 52, 58
Weight 31, 32, 34, 35, 37, 39, 42
Weight sensing................32
Weil, Andrew 12
Wigman, Mary.................3
Wring....................39, 89

Y

Yield & Push ...19, 22, 24, 85, 86, 87

About the Author

Dr. Lisa A. Billingham is Associate Professor of Choral Music Education and Director of Graduate Studies for the Department of Music at George Mason University. She conducts the University Chorale and teaches undergraduate and graduate courses in choral music education. She also gives private instruction in conducting as well as Laban Movement Theory. She is an active member of the American Choral Directors Association, Music Educators National Conference, and College Music Society.

As a Certified Laban Movement Analyst, Billingham's research focuses on the application of Laban Movement Theory to conducting pedagogy and the choral rehearsal. She is active as a clinician and guest conductor for conferences and choirs throughout the United States and abroad.

Dr. Billingham holds a DMA in Choral Conducting from the University of Arizona, an MM in Choral Conducting from the University of Missouri-Kansas City Conservatory of Music and a BME in Choral Music Education from Indiana University (Bloomington). Her conducting mentors include Bruce Chamberlain, Eph Ehly, James Jordan, Maurice Skones, and Volker Hempfling.